Summer Harvest

Brian Brock
Summer Harvest
New & Selected Poems

Acknowledgements

Many thanks to Dr Graham Rowlands for his extensive work reviewing published and unpublished poems, selecting and ordering this collection.

Poems first appeared in *Catharsis* (Pioneer Books, June 1981); *May-Day!* (Pioneer Books, March 1985); *Autumn Peonies* (June 1996); *Spring Gleanings* (Pioneer Books, September 2000); and *Hunters' Place: Smith's Rd, Tharwa* (Ginninderra Press, December 2012).

I would like to acknowledge Chris Ingleton and my daughter Trish Brock for proofreading the manuscript and especially my son, Steve Brock, for keeping me on track and ensuring the completion of the project.

Thanks to Matthew Hunter for the front cover photo featuring kangaroo grass.

Special thanks also to Stephen Matthews of Ginninderra Press for publishing the book.

To John, Angus, Peter, Beth, Margaret
and their families.

Summer Harvest: New & Selected Poems
ISBN 978 1 76041 956 1
Copyright © text Brian Brock 2020
Cover photo: Matthew Hunter

First published 2020 by
GINNINDERRA PRESS
PO Box 3461 Port Adelaide 5015
www.ginninderrapress.com.au

Contents

Foreword	9
Summer Harvest	
Soliloquy	17
Worry Stone	20
The Wutong Tree	22
Broken Hill's Monoliths	23
Confession	24
2 August 2002	25
Adelaide Reconciliation Day	27
Orienteering	31
Backyard Astronomy	32
5.15 a.m. May Day 2002	35
Voyeur, 11.35 p.m. 13 January 2003	36
WW Astronomy Barbecue, 17 June 2001	37
Maya's Birthday Party	38
Sunday, 8 April 2001	41
Poets Incommunicado	43
Bordertown, 14 June 2001	44
Bordertown, 24 November 2002	45
18 February 2006, 5.40 a.m.	46
ANZAC Day, 2004	47
Radiotherapy	50
Clever Fellas	52
Catharsis	
Daybreak	57
Broken Silence	58
Kaurna People	61
Michael	62
Rainstorm on Koki Bay	64
Bombay	65
Sic	67
Nsefu Game Park, 1966	69
The Cormorant	72

For Isobel	73
Torrens Kites	75
Rabbit Trappers	76
Murrumbidgee South of Tharwa	79
Lake Gairdner	81
Yandinga Gorge	83
The Dream	86
Maize Island	88
Tawny and Boobook	91
Murray View	93
The View	94
Credibility Crisis	96
Martindale Hall	97
Festival Felucca	98
Sally	99
Organic	100
to j.c.	101
Gus	103

May Day!

Dear Laurie	107
Aldinga Reef	109
Coorong Samphire	111
Dear Gerry	112
The Kitchen Streaky Bay, 1943	114
Swansea, 3 September 1983	116
Oxford	120
Vienna	121
Paris	122
Desert Hiroshima	123

The Fourth Quarter

The Executioners	127
Beijing's Martyrs' Square	128
Peace Park, Adelaide, 4 June 1990	129
Diamonds	130

Mirror Waters	131
God's Necklaces	133
SEG '90 Moves Out, 12 July 1990	135
Troubridge Island	136
Blue Moon	139
Dear Gus	141
Us (To J.B.)	142

Autumn Peonies

Cape du Couedic	145
War Years, Streaky Bay	146
Marine Archaeology Seminar	148
Night Dive, Edithburgh	150
Peregrine	151
South Hummocks	153
Torrens Bankers	155
Cooper Creek Northwest Branch	156
Smithy's Place	160
Coongie	162
Tiananmen Square	166
Tjilbruke Trail	167
Gretchen – RIP, 3 March 1992	170
Lizean Spitfire	171
Fox Glacier, 19 December 1986	172
Tenth IBA Conference, Wellington	173
Mismatch	175
Kikuyu	176
Wotzke's Window	177
Lorraine and I	178
Signs of Spring	179
Tongues	180
One For Jeff	181
Veale Gardens, 08.50 Hours, 20 May 1991	182

Spring Gleanings

Wellington	187

The Visit	188
Morning Light	190
Kero Lanterns	191
Scones For Tea	192
Babysitting Maya at Julie's Place	194
Coming Out	196
Light	197
Adelaide Heatwave Morning	198
Despite the Rain	200
Maize Island Revisited	201
Wilmington, 19 May 1999	204
Supernova 1987A	207
To John Olday	209
ANZAC Monday, 1999	210
Peace March 1999	212
To Shirley Ackehurst	214
Dulcie May Perry	216
When I Was Five	219

Hunters' Place Smith's Road, Tharwa

Tinderries	223
Murrumbidgee, South of Tharwa	226
Early Riser	228
Silvery Moon	230
Foxing	231
Frank's Place	232
Monday 27 January 2003	233
Monday 27 January 2003	234
Wednesday 29 January 2003 (early a.m.)	235
Wednesday 29 January 2003 (continued)	236
Cryptic Rainbows	237
Merino	238
Rhonda's Poem	239
Neale's Funeral	241
Hunters' Hill	243

Foreword

Brian Brock's opening poem, 'Soliloquy', brings to me so many elements of the themes that will come again and again throughout this collection of his poems. We know the place, White Cliffs. So often we will know the place he loves. And chooks. He begins with chooks. Makes them human. Hears their wake-up call in the dark. Identifies the stars. Comments on changes from the past – exotic peppertrees where 'once mulga'. He is up before dawn. So often he will be up early, maybe with a cuppa. This time coffee, to look into the sky, see the stars, name them, worry if he misses one. See in 'Backyard Astronomy' 'more than this world dreams of'. (He loves Venus, calls her the Diva.) But here before dawn, he is calling.

> Come sun
> pink those breasts.

Galahs. The sun will pink the breasts of all the birds with the colour it brings at dawn. And look at it. 'Pink' is no longer an adjective. It is now a verb. How often that will happen in this collection is one of the delights I find. Laconic. Succinct. See how it works in 'Light'. But, now, as dawn comes, he has 'pink at last'. Now a colour, a noun.

Sharing what he knows, he sees green, not the 'green flash' that I have seen. That touch of physics that is magic. This is what every child can know when he and she bring the colours of blue and yellow together. I know the wonder he shares of that moment and the wonder of making a new colour by mixing two different ones.

In the next poem, 'Worry Stone', he names the member of the clan, 'Ngurna Man'. He has moved from the connection with the past, in the changing landscape of trees, to the human being in a human past, before copper was brought from the mines via Mintaro to the Wakefield River. He has brought in colonisation. He speaks to him. Asks the question, 'Were you the knapper?' We could pass over this technical term or find out what it means and discover he has taken us into the language of archaeology and the human actions needed to make this worry stone. The questions he asks take us to what might have happened, very human actions – but now skimming stones to make them skip across the water – since 'white kids' got here.

He feels all the changes from this memory of the Ngurna to the sailors loading, the muleteers bringing the copper to the vessels. And now the 'ketches have gone'. We have felt the changing times. No words wasted in the process. Again precision. 'Ketches' not just boats. Leaving behind 'stone skippers' and 'developers', he returns to Ngurna Man.

> You've told me your story
> through your knapped-edged worry stone.
> Perhaps that is enough.

Perhaps it is and perhaps it is not. Brian will come back to the past a number of times. He will be more explicit. We find in 'Adelaide Reconciliation Day, 12 June 2000', he is up early again, wondering where Venus is. He decides this is 'A good day for attending to dirty linen whether national or personal.' It's there for us to take in or not take in. He goes on,

> I hang it at dusk
> Graham Rowlands's assurances in my ears:
> 'It will dry;
> if not today,
> tomorrow.'

Reading all Brian's poems, I feel the quality of his precision and wish I had it. I know I am repeating myself but I love the precision in his verbs, sharing his close observations of movement. This precision is there in each poem. And with it shared humanity. And his sense about the depth of the connection. In 'Broken Hill's Monoliths', we feel the dynamic geological past in

> ancient ocean grindings of
> primordial mountains.

Then grandfather. Such a seventh birthday party for Maya. Grandfather. Family. Son. Colleague. And that Scottish inheritance. But often, he is friend. Read the letters. One to a friend who has died. He is very much a country boy and country man. (The city has little place in the collection. Except when he is in Wellington, Oxford, Vienna and 'grey Paris'.) In 'Neale's Funeral', he is talking to a fellow poet, telling him what he would have liked about his funeral.

> Your grandchildren played on the pile
> and helped fill in the grave
> commenting,
> 'There's room for us too.'

This conversational tone is often here. With it, his wry humour. A dry humour most of the time. But he can be angry. His anger is there when he speaks of our actions in 'Clever Fellas'.

> We
> are very clever.
> We can deliver
> seven-ton daisy-cutters
> with precision
> for the excision
> of friends and foes.

Feel the indictment. We are made to feel all we are capable of. Our complicity in it all. What we can do with artillery shells, nukes, machetes, ICBMs. All we can do. His anger is palpable. We can deliver uranium. And 'If the people cannot eat bread let them eat our yellow cake.'

This poem ends the first quarter. The second quarter is 'Catharsis' and he returns to the impact of war in 'Broken Silence' with his father,

> Who survived the Turks
> And diseases
> Of Egypt.

His father is speaking to him, reliving his life and all he did. Who 'set standards impossibly high'. Now, he speaks to his son through words: his words and the words of other men on 'crumbling papers' and 'my memories'.

'Kaurna People' speak to him. Brian is unhappy, feeling what they see. He feels outrage. 'Desert Hiroshima' – such a demanding connection – takes us to Maralinga and Menzies and the politicians who 'sphinx through their terms of office'. The radiation of the First Nations of that land. But the first poem in 'Fourth Quarter' is 'The Executioner', which takes the reader to the Old Jackals. Then there is 'Beijing's Martyrs' Square', where he asks,

> Who then
> speaks for the students and teachers
> censured
> by bullets in the back
> or tank treads as they slept
> in Tiananmen Square?

The Old Jackals have conquered Tibet. In the third poem, 'Tiananmen Square', we feel just how terrible have been the actions of these Old Jackals: 'they crushed and ate their pups'.

There is passion and there can be irony. So much packed in so little in descriptions. In 'Cooper Creek North-west Branch', I'm with him calling pelicans 'Sunderlands or galleons'. The Sunderland takes us to those beautiful planes landing on water, doing such service during World War II. And 'galleons'. Flocks of them. Not the Spanish Armada but great floating power houses with great beauty. Words trigger connections. This time they speak to history.

I find these triggers throughout Brian's poetry. For a time, I thought 'Troubridge Island' would take me to the heart of his poetry. So much is there. The sense of place. There with birds and paints. And the RSM. Who is he? The Regimental Sergeant Major. Precision. Discipline. Regimentation. He is back in the past, as a 'Nasho'; perhaps when all young men had to do national service after 1945. Troubridge Island has a lighthouse. They are above it: this is an aerial view. The passengers feel it

> deep in our being
> as we plane down
> at Edithburgh.

So much of this collection, all of it, is deep in his being. The father, son, biologist, poet, friend, lover of life – past, present and, in Maya, the future.

But in the next poem, 'Blue Moon', he takes me to Roland Robinson. And a group of poets resented by some for appropriating First Nations culture. In fact, I went back to the Jindiworobaks and Roland Robinson's poem 'One-Eyed Nalul Speaks' to 'Balanda' – us the white Australians – 'this is not your country'. I do not see this group as appropriators of First Nations culture. They were ahead of the rest of us, waking to the glory of this land, knowing, as Robinson shows here, long before the Referendum, 'this is not your country'. In the 1930s we had Nazi sympathisers in South Australia in 5KA. (Interesting discovery: 'Future prime minister Robert Menzies, after a visit to Germany in 1938, wrote that the "abandonment by the Germans of individual liberty…has something rather magnificent about it".') In *Kangaroo*, D.H. Lawrence made clear the depth of our racism. But these poets were giving the First Nations their due, although they might feel, as so many did, that they were 'smoothing the dying pillow'. It is not surprising there is sadness. (I invited Ian Mudie to share his poetry with a group of Brighton Boys Technical High School boys in 1975.) If it is part of a poet's job to wake a reader to possibilities and to encourage both the felt and thoughtful response, Brian does it in spades.

There is erudition. Humboldt is here. So is Leibnitz. (I know of Leibnitz through 'the calculus wars' between him and Newton.) Copernicus and Kepler. But this is a scientist-poet who has moved beyond academia. In 'ANZAC Day 2004', he is engaged in

> the war for knowledge
> not just bookish theories.

'In Tawny and Boobook', I do like the boobook 'bobbing his scholastic brow'. I wonder where wisdom lies. Here is passion, precision, close observation. So much deep in Brian Brock's being.

Erica Jolly
May 2020

Summer Harvest

Soliloquy

White Cliffs dawning.
Charlie Orpington heralds the day.
Then Billy Bantam.
Cross and Scorpio dip out.
Communication Tower red lights
beckon and warn the day.
Mercury pinpricks sienna.
Noisy campers leave.
Early gougers beat the sun to Eldorado.
Tree-silhouette horizon
breaks with tradition:
gum and peppertrees
where once mulga dominated.

It's a proud town.
Numbers are down
but long may it last.
Eagles Nest and its northern rival
a blower and power poles
sodium and mercury lights
continue the line.
We're on the grid, we're on the grid,
we're on the grid, we're on the grid.
The solar dishes are redundant.

Magpie calls once.
There's not much competition
in Gwen's gazebo
at this hour.
I wonder why?

A lone cloud in the south-west
but no drought-breaker.
Orange in the east.
My pannikin tea's done.
Will I greet sunrise,
or bow to the superior intelligence
of nipped fingers?
Cross and Scorpio fade.
A generator rattles on Sullivan's Hill.
Lights surge on.
A chill zephyr blows,
but not enough to turn the Freelight.

Come on sun.
I can't wait all day.
Put a bit of sparkle
in those opal chips!

Nose and fingers feel the nip
despite gloves.
I'll deserve some Brownie Points.
The first thirty black galahs
wing in in tight formation.

Coffee calls
but so does seeing the sun rise.
The early start and huge mullock heaps
must mean something.

Edmund Francis Murphy
1862–1950.
I take a turn
to the honeyeaters' mistletoe tree.
Too early.
Charlie has another go.
Nine more galahs,
+2, +4, +1.
Erratic descent to their flight room
for the day's briefing.
18, 10, 3, 3, 50.
Come on sun;
pink those breasts!
Buckets rattle on the diggings.
Tony has stirred.
His coffee is a better bet than rain.

Pink in the east at last.
I would even agree about the green,
but probably from yellow on blue
rather than a green flash.
Another gouger wanders off.
More galahs wing by the rising sun.
I'll not wait for outer warmth.
A vote for coffee.

Worry Stone

Ngurna man
I've found your worry stone
slipping down the white clay years
of this Wakefield River bank.
Were you the knapper?
Did your thumb worry this smoothness
and drop it?
Or did some white kid
find your flint
and skip it across flood tide
into red samphire
there to lodge and lie
as tides and tides
and padding feet and fox
wore the bank away?
Should I let it lie
and slowly slide
into the deep of flood and ebb?

Now it is my worry stone
knapped edges
etched ridges
long to warm in my hand
on a cold night
as I think of the Ngurna
and sailors
and copper muleteers.
The ketches have gone.
So too rails, sheds and wheat stacks.

Your worry stone will outlast me
and a thousand more generations
of whitefellas
or blackfellas
or yellowfellas.

Ngurna man
maybe I'll throw your worry stone
far across the samphire
into the setting sun
beyond the reach of Wakefield floods
or stone skippers
or developers.
You've told me your story
through your knapped-edged worry stone.
Perhaps that is enough.

The Wutong Tree

I return to Morialta
listening to water flowing
amongst quartzite boulders
and watching birds.
I find the Wutong tree…
an ancient pink gum
by the path
dead half from the Kaurna dynasty
live half-flowering now
for honeyeaters
and passers-by.

Thanks He Zhu
for your Song dynasty poem
and Mr Kung for translating…
allowing me to see
Morialta's Wutong tree,
living link with Kaurna ancestors.

Mr Kung Ching Hao uses 'Wutong' in his translation of He Zhu's poem on page 103 of *Modern Rendition of Selected Old Chinese Ci-Poems (1999)*.
Mr Xu Yuan Zhong calls it a 'plane tree' in his translation of He Zhu's poem on page 219 of *Song of the Immortals An Anthology of Classical Chinese Poetry (1994)*.
Morialta: perhaps a corruption of what may have been a Kaurna word 'moriatta' meaning 'ever flowing' – NPWS.

Broken Hill's Monoliths

for Jason (our bus driver)

mulga-tufted hills
guard the sculptures
mother and child
dreamed
and pained out of sandstone
straining up
now
and for the next thousand years
sandstone monoliths
great blocks
quarried and carted here
from ten-thousand-year *old country*
where the People lived for thousands of years
until chilled out
into this *new country*

ancient ocean grindings
of primordial mountains
cemented and raised again
weathered down
monoliths
set in place on sculpture hill
and slowly wrought
by people of many cultures
gifts from culture to culture
for long time
until weathered down again
by the same mountain grinding elements

Confession

Dear Annie,
I've had another good day in the bush
thanks to your teaching
(we observed and absorbed).
Don't know where the racism bit came from.
Certainly not from you or Susie or Jacky,
our mentors from nought to eight.
Maybe a year of primary school 'wisdom' sufficed.
I remember clearly
the second and circumstance
of first hearing and taking up the taunt.
You were returning along Doctor's Beach
perhaps from finding pigface in the dunes.
We were impregnable
Kings of the Castle
on top of the tea tree shelter shed,
until we saw the thunder on your face.
We scampered off and hid in a great heap of tree limbs
lopped by council
and freshly dumped near the beach.
Hide from lifelong tracker Annie?
Your thunder
and shaking digging spear
inches from our cheeky noses
put us off racist taunts
for life.

2 August 2002

Dear Mum,
Been thinking of you this morning.
Just brought in a bandage
from the fencing wire line
I strung up under the carport
because of the rain.
Rolled the bandage on my knee
like I saw you do many times
when we were in the wars
and our brothers were in the islands
battling the Japs.

Saw the Devon Downs shelter yesterday
where you did your dig
with whoever was doing the dig
and your young Cilento friend.
Mrs Hunter showed us 'round…
a brief look before our U3A trip.
Cess Rigney was the site boss
but Cynthia and Raelene
reckoned they could keep him under control
as they edged him over from each side
while he sipped his coffee.
They were waiting for the Princess
but she was exercising her regal prerogative…
running half an hour late.

Thanks Princess.
You gave us time with Cynthia
and her amazing knowledge of the symbols
and layering of sediments and artefacts
and methods of dating them.
Long-necked Kadaitcha Man
was the big boss.
Long-necked tortoise and Beaky
good tucker.

Not for me to tell you much.
I'm not the keeper of the stories.
All those years of driving past
along bleak cleared mallee roads
and not knowing what you knew
was down the cliffs.

I'll go back in spring
with the U3A mob
and hear more of Cynthia's story,
'bout the symbols
and red, white, yellow, and black bands
in the hearths of the people
who sheltered here by their cooking fires
looking out over the river
as the rains and orange sands
trickled down.

Adelaide Reconciliation Day

12 June 2000

'A crisp morning in Adelaide'
to quote the radio weatherman.
I cold-foot it outside
to see the planets.
Think Venus has returned
heralded by edgy Saturn.
Just as well I renege
on ringing my astronomer mate
at six a.m. holiday time;
it is Jupiter,
though I discern no moons
in the lightening sky.
Later
a close reading of rising and setting times
tells me why Venus is so elusive:
it is too close to the sun to see.

A good day for attending to dirty linen
whether national or personal.
In the event
I hang it at dusk
Graham Rowlands's assurances in my ears:
'It will dry;
if not today,
tomorrow.'

I opt for the march
not the wash trough.
Sign on early.
Not many takers at ten a.m.
Time to inspect Hercules
and wonder at the 'baubles'
half hidden in his right hand;
crush a camphor tree leaf
and savour its smell;
read Vic's eulogy
on the figurined gates;
circle and admire
the Smithy biplaned monument,
and drift back to Vic's road.

Wonder if we will get five hundred.
Meet G.R.
and talk Box Factory
poets
and life experiences.
Think we could get a few thousand.
The crowd grows
waving hand cutouts
and occasional banners and flags.
Even the dogs flag support.

Move off at last.
Must be ten thousand.
Plenty of children
and elders
and in betweens.
Cross the city bridge
and break for the rotunda.
Twenty-five minutes later
the column is still streaming from Vic's road.
I up my estimate to twenty-five thousand.
Then we are told forty,
and fifty-five.

Stirring
and more political speeches
vocals and accompaniments
Torres Strait Islander
with headdress
paint
bow and arrow
and song and dance.
New generation declaration.
Good vibes.

G.R. goes.
I spot five of my favourite ladies
in the last five minutes
but tie my kangaroo down.

My turn to wander away.
I pause towards the oval end of the bridge,
lean on the parapet and rest my feet,
watching paddleboaters
fountain
rotunda
latticed crane on building site
flapping ducks
sedate swan
rippling water
and writhing white snakes
slither-swimming into pilings.
Trace them
to lighted side
of skeletal winter poplars
reflected in grey water.

Rotunda action subsides.
I follow the standard bearer
towards the cathedral
and catch my bus.
The washing waits.

Orienteering

I've been up early
orienteering
on the moon.
It is not really upside down.
My Leibnitz Mountains
were three-quarters of a moon away…
probably Mare Humboldtianum's
ridgy inner wall
silhouetted against a dark slip of 'sea'.

I almost one-upped Annie Oakley.
Would have with uncluttered horizons.
I'll try again tomorrow.
The moon will slip back
and the sun will rise earlier.
Then Annie,
I've got the *sun and the moon*
in the morning
and the stars at night.

Backyard Astronomy

Dear Dariell,
You are right,
the Hills hoist
is an important orienteering point
for my backyard astronomy.
This morning
I see the Cross is clear from here.
Jupiter and two of its moons
and the Leibnitz edge of our moon
best from the back door.
Saturn,
in its current triangular juxtaposition
with Aldebaran and Betelgeuse
centroids the neighbour's almond tree.
With the Sisters set
Venus ought to be considering her entry.
On tiptoes
by the far corner of the garage door,
I strain for a glimpse of the 'Star'.
Too early,
but her agent Mars
has checked in.
It is pleasantly cool outside.
Even the pavers
are pleasantly cool under bare feet;
a relief from the day's 'stinking heat'.
Venus must have made her resplendent arrival
by now.
I'll check again.

It is 4.10 a.m.
There she is,
a thumb's width above the horizon,
her agent a thumb's width precedent.
('Dear Mister Precedent.')

4.20
Prime viewing time.
Venus two thumb widths up.
A high-flying jet
gatecrashes the Cross.

4.35
A west to east satellite
glides past Jupiter,
clearing the top of a neighbour's pine.
A breathless zephyr
does not even stir the almond's leaves.
My sole tells me
I am standing in the day's shadow.
I plot the pattern of cool and warm pavers,
and enjoy inhaling the cool air.

There is more to backyard astronomy
'than this world dreams of…'
but I 'will hafta'
clean up the half-bricks and cardboard
I stub my toes on.

PS 4.57 a.m.
A very bright satellite
heads south towards Mars-Venus,
'switching' off before passing between them.

PPS 5.09 a.m.
I have been waiting for a meteor.
Zoom in to inspect the moon again
through almond twigs and leaves.
Keep moving
to dissuade little black ants and mosquitoes.
The dawning sky lightens.
No luck with meteors.
The plane of Jupiter's moons has tilted.
Venus seems pretty full.
The Breathalyser Squad will not be pleased.
My breath?
Tea.

PPPS 5.35 a.m.
The fullish moon
settles down below the almond boughs.
Jupiter, Venus, Sirius, Canopus, linger.
Blackbirds forage.
Venus will soon be the Diva.

PPPPS 6.01 a.m.
The Diva takes centre stage.

PPPPPS 6.07 a.m.
The sun rays the east.

5.15 a.m. May Day 2002

Nev's birthday.
Robin's obit in *Mesa*.
Port Wakefield samphire trail day.

The moon
is five fingers north of Scorpio's sting.
I've been using binoculars
to look at crater wall mountains
along the rough edge of the gibbous moon
silhouetted on the shadow of the long lunar night.
Seas of tranquillity.
Splash lines of light
radiate from Copernicus and Kepler.
Aristarchus flares.
An earth satellite glides past.
Bare feet feel the cold of patio pavers.

Voyeur, 11.35 p.m. 13 January 2003

Quick!
Get your binoculars.
The gibbous moon
sports a little nipple
on her sagging breast
at this phase of her cycle.

WW Astronomy Barbecue, 17 June 2001

Sunshine milk is the nectar of the gods
after a l-o-n-g d-a-y.
Mars
Scorpion
Southern Cross
satellites
and shooting stars.
What more could one want
after Coorong mullet entree
and tea beside the brazier?

4.35 a.m. 18 June 2001
I've caught the crescent moon
Cheshire grin and craters
through whispy cirrus.
I'll have to run a dawn course in astronomy
to show her elusive smile.
Little finger later
Venus is here.
No wonder the moon is content.
Mallee coals glow down
in my brazier.

Maya's Birthday Party

Canto One

Pied Piper Trish
races down the hill
flying a yellow jellyfish kite
tentacles streaming and rippling and twisting.
The captured crocodile of party guests
girls' long dresses
swishing and brushing green grass
follows the piper around the paddock
with shouts of glee.
Up to the top of the hill
all to have a turn
racing down the hill
jellyfish dipping and diving
around the trees
and back up the hill.
Yellow jellyfish kite
bonding
bonding.

Canto Two

'Grandpa
you can look after the fire and damper
and please bring the marshmallows.'
Grandpa is happy to oblige.
but has to think a bit
about how best to organise all this:
stoneground wholemeal plain flour
sultanas
mixing bowl and wooden spoon
cutting board
water
and green bamboo sticks
to wind damper snakes around.
I harvest my bamboo crop
cut convenient lengths
and trim and clean.

Canto Three

Yellow jellyfish kiting exhausted
the children rested.
Grandpa chose a fire site
and soon the stringy bark and wattle blazed.
The snakes objected to the coiling
so dough was squeezed and moulded.
Around the coals the dough girls gathered
twirling dough until sultanas popped.
Ease the damper from the stick
blowing through to make it cool.
Load the cylinder with honey
even watching magpies drool.

Marshmallows melt and flare on sticks.
Eat them while they're soft and warm.
Prezzies next and then the cake.
Thread the needle guard of honour.
Maya takes the pride of place.
Hers the blowing of the candles.
Hers the wish when cutting cake.
Stir the fire as stars appear.
Children gather sticks and leaves
feeding theirs with supervision
till ghosts come 'round the darkening scene.
So we leave the lovely party.
Maya's seventh
has come and been.

Sunday, 8 April 2001

It was the *rats* day in Brisbane;
Bright's day in Adelaide;
The Crows licked three-point wounds.
Nephew Peter paid a rare visit,
armed with Scarpantoni and Bleasdale Cab Sav.
On Clipsal Eve we toasted the Pottses…
winemakers, shooters and mathematicians supremo;
also good times on Maize Island.

Peter boxed on at the big race.
Trish and Maya enjoyed Grandpa's cantata: Olivet to Calvary.
Maya helped plan our day:
a tow to BP for the paper, Mum pulling the trolley;
Grandpa harnessed later, did too many wheelies;
back to the straight and narrow,
which means crabwise,
until I fix those back wheels.
Maya honed more skills in the backyard:
grinding lavender and lemon verbena
for mosquito repellant
sawing wood
hammering straight
and discovering vices;
learning about paddle-wheeled outriggers
trialled in the bath;
made herself a little kite from a modified recipe,
drinking straw frame
love heart decorations
wool on her patent reel.

I hung the kite on her Goodies Tree
ate all the spare Anzac biscuits
(still two on the tree;
come quickly if you want your share)
microwaved my three dried figs
(to soften them and kill the crawlies).

The race over
Peter bussed 'home' and opted for Berri.
Trish and Maya reluctantly headed for the hills.
Curly Playground will have to wait.
Palm Sunday's moon outshone Mars Probe Three,
promising low low tides for my U3A beach walk.
Perhaps I'll hear Poetry Under the Pier.
I rescue recent plantings from slugs and snails.
Be warned you ravenous molluscs,
I'll treat you to Heavy Rock.
Your ravages abated once you were slated.

Poets Incommunicado

we pass in the square
play solitaire

Bordertown, 14 June 2001

That
is a sound I know.
Cathy's rooster crows
as the moon switches on and off
through patchy cloud.
Semis hammer the highway.
The emu drums.

5.20 a.m.
Cathy's roosters
sequentially call up the day.
I coax the night's embers into flame
fiddling and feeding
and gently breathing.
The reluctant ironbark
flickers and splutters.
I recruit twigs and leaves
and big gun mallee stump
and note the roosters' calls are working.
My back turned
the fire flares.
I warm bare legs and enjoy my morning cuppa.

Bordertown, 24 November 2002

Yesterday's heat has eased.
Rain gently arrived
patterning rings
on Cathy's pool.
I take my tea outside
to smell rain
on summer's dry grass.
Four galahs
settle in the skeletal gum
in the Pigman's paddock.
It is the lone partner
of a bookend pair;
no Wutong here,
both long dead;
one recently felled for firewood.

Corellas call from afar.
Lorikeets fly high and fast.
Bully-calf Herefords
wander over for a morning talk,
brown eye-patch 'Pirate'
the friendliest.
Rooster
claims his waveband
with repeated call-signs.
Willy
flits and prances
decoying me from her spiderweb nest.

Time to refill that cup.

18 February 2006, 5.40 a.m.

The boys had to go to war:
'Patriotic German-Australians.
Young men of Tanunda
who have volunteered
for active service abroad.'
(*The Adelaide Chronicle,* p. 29, 6 November 1915)

No mention of the Scot genes.
They were German by propaganda,
despite being third generation Australians.
The heritage of their Murray Walers
both to die under Turkish bombardment,
was not questioned.

Some of the ten Tanunda boys
did not return;
the Brock two,
sick or wounded,
did.

Never a word of the rotten war.

ANZAC Day, 2004

In two minds:
whether to go or no
not having served overseas
in that capacity.
Fought the other war
in Papua and Africa,
Pitjantjatjara lands
and Adelaide.
The war for knowledge.
Marvels and mysteries of Science;
seeing and doing,
not just bookish Theories.

ANZAC Day 2004.
Prospect Dawn Service
and rummy coffee.
Hadaway
the Burma Star man,
and other Vets there,
and spic and span cadets.
Bought my badge
from the veteran badge-best-seller.

Free bus to town
dangling my Nasho medal.
Met a few I knew (from HQ Branch)
and a few I didn't.
Two from Booleroo.
Cooky from the Riverland
where I first learnt the ropes:
.22 .303 Owen Bren Piat.
Thousands of rounds later
'I don' 'ear so good.'
Those dedicated Good Guys
Balls Baldwin and Ernie Hayden
regularly tripped to Glossop
to help Bill Barret
with his unit.

The ANZAC wait dragged on.
Sore back.
Sore feet.
Why was I here?
The bands were good.
The Lone Piper did his round.
Our turn at last.
We swung away
and raggedly wheeled;
d-islocations
m-oved d-own t-he r-anks.
Flags waved.
The crowd encouraged us.
Babies slept.

We did our eyes rights
and eyes fronts
and kept step
past the dais
where Marj got an accolade
from her troops.

Disbanded by the big fig.
We had remembered.

Radiotherapy

Dear John,
Been talking to Beth and Suzie
in Germany.
Maddie 'talked' too.
So did the little heart patient
from the Ukraine
climbing dangerously in the background.

Here,
the crescent moon
sank through the almond tree
west of the Sisters and Aldebaran.
No doubt his red eye
featured in your Mustang navigation.
Pity your last flight
was such a spectacular disaster.
Not every pilot tips over a patrol dozer
with his Mustang.
At least it spared you
from Hiroshima's lingering radiation.
Your young brother was not so lucky.
He told me a bit
one long trucky trip to Victoria Market.
Wouldn't be many of them left:
the Occupation Forces overdosed in Hiroshima,
or the radiation guinea pigs
of Monte Bello and Emu Fields.

Your youngest sister outlived you slightly,
stricken with the congenital big C.
I'm the next test case.
I'll be radiant
after five days a week for seven and a half weeks.
At least I won't be vapourised
like Hiroshima's 'disappeared'.
Pinochet's thugs
could have learnt something from Hiroshima.
Unlike Angus, they missed the enlightenment.

Clever Fellas

We
are very clever.
We can deliver
seven-ton daisy-cutters
from a great height
with precision
for the excision
of friends and foes.

We
are very clever.
We can blow down mountains
and deliver artillery shells
and Nukes
across the Himalayan foothills
with precision
onto schools and markets
and even the occasional army post.

We
are very clever.
We can kill a million fellow citizens
using only machetes.

We
are very clever.
We can launch satellites
and lob ICBMs
with precision
beyond Japan.

We
are very clever.
We can leaky-leach uranium
and go underground in huge trucks
for copper and gold
and even more uranium.
We can deliver.
If the people cannot eat bread
let them eat our yellowcake.
We can deliver
five minutes after pressing the button
but bread
within a week of Goma
or any other catastrophe
is expecting a bit much.

We
are very clever.
Ask the Woomera lip-sewers.
They know
but find it difficult to articulate.

Catharsis

Daybreak

(from a hospital bed)

Irregular undulations of cloud
Slowly drift across the horizon
Of my notebook page of sky.
Darker hills
To softer grey give way
As a sparrow's flitting scribble
One corner
Inscribes
And the rest of the page
Pales into day.

Broken Silence

So
Father
You talk to me
Talk to me down these sixty years
Through crumbly yellowed newspapers
South Eastern Times
Of the early twenties.
Handwritten journal reports
From the Mount
When you and Grimes
Rode the craters
And shorelines
Patrolling
And exercising and breaking horses
Thomas Elder's mongrel greys from Marree
Murray Waler packhorses from Kidman's river properties.
You had to be tough
To be a PIG
Then
Breaker Brock.
You
Who survived the Turks
And diseases
Of Egypt
In World War One
Had other battles
With men
And fear
To come.

Fear almost drowned you
Deep in Crater Lake
Jammed beneath a tree
With a dead boy's body.
That fear
And cold
And pain of water pressure
Haunted you
Until lesson twelve
From the Pelman Institute
In 1923 –
In your own hand: 'I confidently believe I am fearless.'
No fear of mad mobs
Or poison gas in well
Or horse
Or snake
Or shark infested waters
Or armed men
Or bush.

You who survived Turk
And mosquito-borne diseases
In Egypt.
You
Who escorted kings and princes
Through Adelaide's streets
And paraded in Canberra
In 1927
Representing the South Australian Mounteds
At the opening of Parliament House.

You
Who loved babies
And sunset over water
The smell of shotgun powder
Milking burping cows
And goats.
You
Set standards impossibly high
But now
You
Silent One
Speak to me
Through this case of crumbly papers
Through your words
And the words of other men
And my memories.

I take the cup
But my hand trembles.

Kaurna People

Kaurna people
this was your land
now concrete, roads and cars
Kaurna people
this was your land
now drifting dunes where once the mallee grew
Kaurna people
these were your living hills
where now the streams are still
or rage in flood
Kaurna people
these were your open spaces
where now the fence confines
Kaurna people
these were your swamps and waterways
where now our garbage lies
Kaurna people
best your spirits dream
than see all this
and die again
as this your land has done.

Michael

We compare map
With this land of your Dreaming
Five thousand feet below.
I read Ayers Rock, Olgas, Mount Connor, Tomkinson Ranges
And other whitefella names.
You read those
And more
That you are allowed to know
Of the Dreaming
But that
We cannot share.

I read signs of rabbit plagues:
Pin-pricked warrens
Of different hue
Set in the grey green
Of this country after rain;
Spinifex country pocked with minute lichen cups;
Dead mulga stubble
Casting black pencil lines across the ground;
Surface water
Brown
Then shimmering ripples
And blaze of light
As we leave it and sun behind;
Brown ribbons of road and survey lines;
Shredded ribbons of dry creekbeds
Fringed with green of river gums.

We swoop over Kalka
And curve around the valley
To Pipalyatjara strip
And hear the Budget talk
And feel the credibility squeeze
And I try to see
Where science fits into this.

Back to Amata.
More Dreaming Country,
Down into the shadows of the valley.

Rainstorm on Koki Bay

Thunder clouds devour the azure blue of Koki Bay
Palms tower above the market
Canoe houseboats
Glean last traces of sunshine beside the causeway.
Frangipani
Heavily scents the air
Competing with fruity market smells
A bus's warning blare
And mission bells.

Regular market squatters and talkers
Check the sky with calculating eye
And plan escape
As large warm drops splash on sticky flesh.
Murky waters brood a while.

Down pours the rain
Sweeping all before
Litter and men.
Market people scatter with their wares
Pedestrians scurry for shelter
Naked children splash through drains into the bay and out again.
All seem happy to see and feel and smell the rain
Elders with betel-stained teeth
Truckloads of plantation workers singing their way home
Urchins in the bay.

The deluge ends.
As evening veils the Koki scene
Cooking fires crown dripping houseboats
And cicadas sing and preen.

Bombay

Multi-storeys
Unfinished
Concrete
Grey;
Rising from waterlogged flats.
QANTAS
Big and ugly hoarding,
Shading out the humpies
Before the narrow shopfronts
On the way to the
Taj Mahal
And the Gateway to India.

Trim gardens
Up on the hill
On the roof of the reservoir
With an old Indian keeper
Full of tradition
And Untouchable
Telling stories
About the sculptured cypresses
The Arabian
And Indian
Oceans.

Sitting in the open-air café
By the cobra charmer
Drinking coke
While the waiter chases crows
(Fresh from picking bones
Of the night's dead)
From the balustrade.

Bombay beach
With its rows of peeling flats
And palms
And taxicabs
And the air-conditioned Taj Mahal
Wheeling the baby in the pusher
By the Gateway to India
Through the throng of vendors
And strollers
Affluent
Touriste
And bloody hot.

Sic

cocos hermit crabs
scavenge between palms
near the ocean
lapping this ten-foot atoll
midnight refuelling stop
en route mauritius

we swelter
watching hermit crabs
watching us
watching them
as they edge into our generated pool of light
and out again
like us

mauritius
dodo island
abrupt peaks
and green of sugar cane
boys at the airport
watching planes come
and go
with france
in thin gold rims
duty-free cigarettes
and eau de cologne on after-dinner tissues
ad nauseam

eau de cologne
and refuelling fumes
and duty-free cigarette smoke
tourist class

nausea
18 hour turbo prop electra nausea
over madagascar
continent island
roc
lemur
laterite

so to joburg
and that other sickness
that makes it god's own country
for god's chosen people
and shareholders in the multinationals

salisbury
bulawayo
livingstone
and the smoke that thunders
freedom thunders too
after the oppression south of the zambesi
i chunder
in the integrated toilet

Nsefu Game Park, 1966

Fishing for barbels
Out on a Luangwa sandbar
Near the impala carcass
Lying there for the crocs
After the lions the night before.
The barbels sulk.
Elephants cross the river
Strung out against sunset red.
Grassfire smoke in the atmosphere.

Lions cough closer
So we pack up
And have a beer
In the eating-house
Watching Egyptian geese
And wattled plovers
While vultures gorge
And carmine bee-eaters
Settle in the sandy cliffs.

Elephants came in the night-time
Quietly.
Great straw-coloured blocks of dung
Stripped mopane trees
And wheel-trapping footprints in baked mud
Testify their existence
Until harvested
By poachers or vets
For ivory
Or meat for the Copperbelt.

Early morning and late afternoon
With khaki uniformed guide
Armed against possible charge of rhino
Bull elephant
Or buffalo.

Whisking tsetse flies
While tracking down hippos
By their deep belly laugh.
Then out past the rhino's sausage tree
Looking for the unpredictable beast
And lining up 'safe' retreats.
We found them
Nibbling bushes and snorting a bit
So left discreetly
Past Kudu statues
On termite-mound pedestals.

Whistling fish-eagles
Wheel above mud holes
Etched by croc slither-tracks
And staked out
By serious marabous.
Racket of waterbirds.

Back to camp
Through scurrying guineafowl
Buck
And protesting baboon troupes –
Leaving the bush night
To the carnivores,
And part of it
To their prey.

The Cormorant

There broods that sleek dripping huntress
Sovereign of her liquid world. Who knows
The thrills, the eagerness, the calm distress
Of a lost chase through translucent flows?

> Through this semi-solid streamlined world
> Of fleeting, flashing, silver fishes
> A jagged, jet thunderbolt is hurled
> With scarce a ripple. Down she swishes;
> With gaping maw, strikes! Her curled

Beak bites deep and flushes the very
Throne of life with the cold, oozing
Blood. Up through chill dreary
Liquid realms she glides, musing

> On future conquests. Greenish, yellow,
> Brighter, lighter grows this medium,
> And faster flees the demon below
> The lifeless silver bream, plucked from
> The heart of the vibrant lagoon. A shower

Of scintillating gold heralded
The thrust from world to world. Now
Gorged with life, she sits in the blood
On an old, dead red-gum bough.

> There in the warm winter sunshine
> She preens her gleaming, greasy plumage.
> How deceptive! So clean and fine
> She seems, this glossy, latent savage.

For Isobel

fingers
fingers tingle
from shifting tiles and bricks
and a thousand crates of accumulated junk
fingers tingle
from shifting house
and scraping barnacles and tube-worms
from the plastic coating
of the wires
supporting tiles
hanging there
under a pontoon platform

fingers hanging here
fifty cm below the surface
fingers and tiles
and barnacles and tube-worms…
assorted marine invertebrates
i wished them well as you requested
hanging here
in the same water
flowing past
clouded with silt
and flecks of life

detached fingers
working there alone in the murk
as fingers have worked
for man
for eons
since fingers first apposed thumbs

fingers working and tingling
in the restricted field
of face-mask vision
as we hang here
together
and alone

tiles
and foulers
and fingers
and i

thinking of you
thinking of me
with fingers tingling

Torrens Kites

hover there
black-shouldered kite
hover there
and watch for ripples in the sea of weeds
where once the celery grew
hover and glide and baulk and hover
black-shouldered kite
watching for mice
amongst the weeds
hover and glide
hover and glide
above it
and of it
the race in the wilderness
above it
and of it
as we are
behind our glass
hovering
and racing
but yet to learn to glide

Rabbit Trappers

Dust, rectangled newspaper, blood,
Guts.
Fur, and broken bones.
Urine; plenty of urine;
Wet near scratches and fresh prints,
Wet on squats –
With plenty of turds.
Dry urine dust when setting squats.
Pale fibrous green of dried pellets
Crushed by the setter.
Sparks from peg;
Metal against metal;
Smell of shattered limestone.
Rattle of chain,
Click of plate,
Gently,
Gently,
Set.

One can be a gentle trapper.
Not too sentimental.
Let the little farts go –
But there's method in that madness.

Cruel?
Traps are cruel
The pain of broken bones is cruel
The fear is cruel
The squeal is cruel
But the death may be kind
The handling of trapped vermin gentle –
Gently lifted by the flank,
Released from the metal vice;
Gently laid across the knee,
Swiftly broken neck.

Heat
Horehound smell
Trapped 'kitten' – broken legs.
Too soft the child
To bear the broken bones
The blood and guts – alone.
Too hot
Too tired
Too sentimental
Too much.

Nights
With brightest moon and brightest stars
Stumbling in the darkness
That only a hurricane lantern makes;
Bobbing flickering darkness,
Darkest near the stumbling feet.
Hurricane lantern kerosene smell.
Smoky smell.
Hot handle in the coldness;
Rectangled *Chronicle* coldness;
Handing papers to the veteran
In the gorges
Up above the mallee patches;
Watching railcars snaking down
To twinkling towns across the blackness.

Murrumbidgee South of Tharwa

Brown falcons, kestrels and ravens
Feed on grasshoppers.
Foxes and starlings also fatten on the plague.
Wombats, roos and sheep
Compete for grass on the highest hills
Where cicadas crowd and choir scraggly Manna gums.
Herefords possess the slopes
Urgently.

We retreat from the heat
To Murrumbidgee rapids, pools and sandy beaches.
Children gather mud-eyes from warm sandbars
Watching dragonflies emerge,
Pump up abdomen and wings
And take first flights from fingertips.

A peregrine falcon
Sweeps past caves
High in limestone cliffs
Settles for a while
In a grey sentinel tree
Until routed by a wagtail.

Yellow-faced honeyeaters
Sing in bottlebrush thickets
As we lunch in scant shade
Where foxes come to drink
Leaving signs for those who learn to read.

The children play with a plastic inflatable
Fish or swim
And check their dragonflies.
I stay dry
Though tempted back
As they dive into the deep pool
From a sloping limestone rock.

A final fling collecting feathers from below the cockies' trees.
Scared by wild pigs the kids return to base
And we prepare for the long climb up the eroded track.
Heat
And ants
Treehoppers
And grazing sheep.

Farewell Murrumbidgee
Dragonflies and peregrine.

Lake Gairdner

Mummified locusts,
scorpions,
sundry seeds
and Forde
out on the salt crust
looking at emu shit
with its bitter quandong seeds.

Salt domes,
islands,
horizon of salt one hundred miles away –
shattered shoreline
red brown porphyry rock
etched at the base
by eons of salt and waves and frost –
great rectangled cracks in the crust,
salty driftlines of insects and seeds.

Pittosporum
willow willow
on the spit
with its mistletoe parasite
flowering and fruiting
sticky seeds sprouting penises on other branches.

Back towards billy tea dune
where red-capped robin sat in mulga grey
above scorpion holes
rabbit squats
and rusty bully cans.

Samphire-edged claypan
raped by rover-tread wheelies
Forde's treaded bootprints
and my soft emu-footed ones
like the roos and the emus before us
we were turned by the fence
the new high one
not the socket-toothed memories of the old one.

So we saw Gairdner's Lake
and wished you were here,
Kaye and Meg and Jill,
for you would have loved it
emu shit and all
like we did.

Yandinga Gorge

At last
in the old Peugeot
with its blown head gasket
and constant oil level
floating on the rising water in the sump…

Camped on the alluvium
past the bore
in a wattle thicket
mist netted spiny honeyeater
and his friends
while bad boy butcher-bird
watched and called and waited
ready to chop chop spiny
or blue wren
or thorny mimicking butcher
to scare big boy Nev away.

Wattle campfire
gum logs to give it a kick
red for Nev
not for me
off the grog
after the Moonaree sands
and the long drive down
east seemed west, west east
dry dams
map not quite right
navigator
fuzzy head
fading track
mallee growing on it
glad to reach the bulldozed bit
to Pine Lodge
ruin.

Yandinga Gorge
giants' causeway a thousand times
but red brown
hexagonal prisms and pavements
pompom rocks (Nev's phrase)
batteries of them
spiked when crystallised
from the red giants' magma.

Correa pollen on spiny's bill
(or was it?)
We climbed
Grevillea birdpods
wattle yellow
astrolome red
then we found it:
acres of pale yellow Correa
on southern aspects.

Pavement rock on the ridges
pompoms aimed across the Gorge
yellow-fronteds near the rockholes
high up in the hills.

Hard to leave pompom rocks
spiny
with correa pollen on your bill
bad boy butcher.

The Dream

Campers
amongst the box trees
old Buick cars near the tents
29 model
according to my dream
and ours
looking younger
although a 26 master six
with father standing there
not saying much.

We walked through the orchard
recently disced
to keep down the weeds
knowing
it was in other hands
and destined to disappear.

Through the trees
we came to vines
and looked down over the rest
dry grass
dead gum-tree branches
lopped from edging stands
to cover sand
drifting in whiter patches
where the pears had been.

We walked on
Father and I
and saw all these photos of him
echoing down the years
deepening lines
but content with all that was
as it was.

And now my memories echo
from cliff to ethereal cliff
each in turn
becoming a cliff
from which the train of memories
echoes on.

Maize Island

Cracked
Concrete irrigation pipes
Hiss high in the air
Arcing into orange-brown splatter patches
On the sand
Between the apricot trees
Softening innocent-weed
And heat
In one glorious 36-hour pee
Genuflecting
With pressure changes
In the tank
On Scotty's hill
Across the swamp
Dictating
Numbers of outlets
Open
Or closed
As we swing the bloody hoe
And furrow irrigate
Trees and vines
On this flood-prone
Nutrient-deficient
Winkie Sand
Ready
For the next flood.

1870
1930
1956
1973–4–5.

Orchard pipelines
Join maize lines
Hammer stones
Mussel shells
And Aboriginal bones.
On the Sand Hill
Where the bones lay
An 1870 box
Indicates that waterline.

Box
River-reds
And nardoo
Select their level
As floods retreat.

Blue-wrens
'Possums
And hop-bush stink-beetles
Colonise
Plantings,
Reverting
To some semblance of 1884
Despite metal and weed artefacts.

Emotional bones
Bleach
Exposed to sun
And rain
That pees in wet splatter patches
On the sand of our dreams.

Tawny and Boobook

Tawny frogmouth calls
From his old gum
Lost in the darkness
Away from my campfire.
Oom-oom-oom.

I listen a while
As the fire flares and dies.
Oom-oom-oom
From the big tree
That used to half-shade
Cars and kids
In apricot summers.

At last I respond to his call
And find him
Ooming on
Peering around
At my torch's glare
But content to sit
And Oom.

I leave him
And stir my fire.

Then boobook starts
Further over
In the pillared gum
From which a great bough
Crashed and crushed
Years ago.

I found him too
Bobbing his scholastic brow
And boobooking his appreciation
In my direction.

Oom-oom-oom.
Boobook! Boobook!

My fire flickers
And smokes
And blackens into ash.

Murray View

The smell of reeds
And clinging mud
A sky that bleeds
And swirling flood
Swaying trees
And crumbling earth
Grimy knees
And homely hearth
Tangy wine
And carefree laughter
Verdant vine
And resting after
Hours of toil –
Demand that we
Regard the soil
As Deity.

The View

Ginsberg saw it
on the jessore road
back in 71
which is why we don't read ginsberg
in fraser's australia 76
ginsberg saw them
malnutrition babies
big heads
expressionless eyes
in the retreat
from east pakistan
on the jessore road
while we debated
whether to expend
½ of 1%
of the gnp
on overseas aid
or war

we opted for war
and kwashiorkor bellies
swelled
on ginsberg's road to jessore
so we don't read ginsberg
because he saw it
in the dysenteric flesh
and flood
on the jessore road
which ought to make us choke
on our sunday chicken
as we debate the relative merits
of 1% gnp on overseas aid
or f111s

we opt for f111s
and chicken on sundays
and kwashiorkor bellies
and malnutrition heads
on the jessore roads
of australia 76
but we don't read ginsberg
because he saw it all
the shit and mud
and expressionless eyes
as we debated
before

Credibility Crisis

I thought it mattered for a while
Whether I left one light on or two
But now I doubt it
There have been too many cracker nights
Big boys' wars
Concordes
Satellites
Prestigious limousines
Stockpiled A-bombs
H-bombs too
Get-rich arms deals
Missile fleets
And cold war armies
For it really to matter much
Whether I leave one light on
Or two.

Martindale Hall

Ghosts of the inegalitarian past
Linger on
In fretting stone
And extremes at ends of speaking tubes
Fireplace surrounds of Madam's room
And Nanny's
And baths.

Know thy place.

Coach-house comforts
Succour spirited beasts
That they may better serve
But here
Stay thy side of the Pale
Scullery maid
And count blessings of sound roof kitchen warmth and austerity.
(Madam lacks the latter).

Elegant time's window
    opens 2–4 Sun.–Wed. 2 bucks
    don't smoke in the grass
    and watch where you pee.
Cows receive special dispensation.

Festival Felucca

Poets' Union festival marquee
Britannic colours belching in the breeze
Grog & epithets
Flood from the rip-off bar
Drowning the occasional line.

The bum-numbing mind-blowing over
We join the ripped
At the grog font.

Making a break
We leave a half-carafe
To quell other sensibilities & cares
Struggling up King William Street with ours.

Pancakes and coffee
Then through the Mall
Strangely lighted and subdued
Until the vacuuming monster comes
Sucking up our solitude
In its mechanical soliloquy.
City Council permits for needing a piss expired an hour ago
So we head for the Railway Station
Past the Governor-General's reinforcements.
We part
And you collide with your *gendarme felucca*.

Sally

Plastic flowers
And colour TV
In a saloon bar
With my black and tan
And bloody reserve.

Bad luck bees
Bad luck Fraser Island
Bad luck communication
And Sally
In your lunch hour
From RAH
Drinking squash
From necessity
Rather than desire.

With your reserve
And squash
And my reserve
And black and tan
We were pretty safe
Watching that colour TV
With its aqua-espionage
Near the plastic flowers
On the saloon bar.

Organic

this is it
life
now
sitting on a banana crate
crunching an organic carrot
from the central market
not the tastiest
but at least organic
whatever that means in australia
it should mean
human excreta
recycled in the commune

i sit
and crunch
and listen to the city traffic
as drivers consummate their unholy alliance
with sacrifices
beneath the moon blob
silhouetting my loquat tree and vines
and the lunatic system
fostering sacrifices
to keep the economy rolling

at least it is organic
the fuel and fumes
and the recycling
of homo driver sapiens
and children

to j.c.

jesus
you called me over
under the cypress tree
in the garden

we talked a bit

i didn't know
but it was your last day

you talked of greece
and being a p.o.w.
they were nice blokes
we didn't take many tricks
in greece

and today was your last day
but i didn't know
even though
we talked a while

the old cock
crowed twice
and three times
before saint john came

i left you with him
under the cypress
in the garden
you knew so well

it was your last day
in the garden
and you wondered why
you fought them
jesus

Gus

Dear Gus
You survived Rabaul
And the Japs
And malaria
And the Geisha Girls
During the Occupation
Relaying the first message
From the still-hot receiving end
Of THE BOMB
Maybe that's why
Cancer's got your kidney now
But who's to know?

It's a long haul
From Coorong barbecues
To Flinders Medical Centre
6 G;
But smell that barbecue
See that Coorong sunset
Smell that shrubby dune
After rain
Right here
In Flinders Medical Centre
6 G
Where we are,
Learning about transcience:
Ours.

Swallows

who are you
who watch the swallows
as i do
close enough
to see the windows in their swallow tails
satiny blue sheen of backs
chestnut brown of breast
occasional fleck of light
on insect pursued
in fluttering rise
and sweeping glide
over sloping lawns
or pools

who are you
who sit in the sun
and follow the swallow
lines and designs
brown windowed wings
full flight dunking splashing washing

there
the swallow
neatly folded
sunning

who am i
neatly folded
i wonder

May Day!

Dear Laurie

If ever a spider was set up
    That one was
As we watched its nocturnal web
    Sway gently
In a breath of air.

    Careful now
Avoid the gossamer stays
    As we watch
And you jockey for the best position
    To capture its aesthetic
        And architectural
            Web
    In projector-lighted clarity.

It was well set up
    And so were we
        Projector
    Daylighting treetops
        And moths
As we got our angles right.

The inevitable happened
    We forgot the web
In our preoccupation with angles:
    Some of it
Drifted high across the garden
    The rest
Was picked from head and beard.

The architect
Escaped with its plans
        We
With our images.

Aldinga Reef

See one reef and you've seen them all
Above the waterline.
Poor old Aldingii has faded a bit
With all those earnest groups
Warrener and crabber turnstones
New storm-water drain
And even a galah in a four-wheel drive
Scarring its surface.

But here below the surface
The protection is more complete:
Man and feet
Drift weightless above the world
        they would destroy in worshipping
        on land.

This dive was a study in kelp brown
Over glorious coralline pink
        painting rock surfaces
Electric-blue fin-edged fish
Iridescent coral
Yellow sponges
Fawn bracketed bryozoans
And feathery hydroids
        swirled gently by the waves
        up there at the cascading mirror
        reflecting me down.

Pale ghost-legged students
Snorkel and soak it in
While I seal swim
Silently working fingered flippers
Like Goose Island's seals
With whom I exchanged ideas
Some years ago.

Gloves and jumper keep me warm
Beneath my wetsuit
But eventually I lumber back to earth
Taking on the usual gravities
After the Impressionistic gallery
Below the waterline.

Coorong Samphire

Through the red samphire
white-fronted chats
and red-capped dotterels
kept their broken-winged distance.
Not deceived
I slowly crossed towards The Coorong
past their young.
Two roos
as slowly hopped along the water's edge.
Downwind
I watched them hop and nibble
and leisurely leap across the clay.

They did not see my yellow raincoat.
But then
they met the wind-stream of man scent.
Shocked surprise!
Whirl and leap and flee
towards the distant dunes.

I looked at the story
freshly told in muddy prints
and slowly arced back
through the chats' samphire.

Dear Gerry

Dear Gerry
We didn't talk much
These last twenty years
Twenty seasons
Of wistaria
And apricot flowers and leaves
As you battled your battles
And I mine.

I'm still battling
And will probably see
These loquats and apricots yellow.
You mate won't
Unless you up there
Scan the whole screen
Of us down here.
One up on us.

Here's a French brandy
To old times
Swinging the hoe on Maize Island
With Innocent weed in our socks
And hot sand burning our feet
While midday port and ice
Made us wonder
Whether we swung hoes
Or hoes swung us
Amongst trees and vines
Of hot summer irrigation.

Latimer, Olday, Schneider, Holzner, Theunissen,
 Nikoloudis, Hall, Sir Francis Roy Thompson:
All those bright buggers
Dance a different tune now
Twenty-five years after the event.

Burn sand
Burn brandy.
Here's to prickly socks
And hoe swung heads
On port and ice
Poured decades ago.

The Kitchen Streaky Bay, 1943

Lemon
grated white
squeezed into cinnamon cake
sprinkled with sugar
salivating sour.

Buttermilk
trickling from the churn
and finding its way
into cut triangles
of brown-topped scones.

Yeast
working away
in the warm window
by the wood stove
on which the big iron water-urn
steamed
stove-pot black
while the week's dough
rose in warm blankets
in a tub on the hearth.

Separator
whining its way up
to tap-turning
cream-running speed.

Steaming tubs of wash-up water
one scalding hot
particularly for milk buckets
and TB germs.

Late night clatter;
smell of burning meths
in the four-pound weight
from the kitchen scales…
singed pin-feather smell
of the night's wild duck bag.

Tall white glass-fronted dresser
with sliding doors
green-ringed plates
banana-shaped two-teated babies' bottle
and vegetable masher
that made piles of worms
children preferred.

Oysters
in bowled batter
near the window.

Mum
in light summer prints.

Swansea, 3 September 1983

Walking forty-five degree-wise
across wind-sculptured sand
to the periwinkled groyne,
and on over water-rounded pebbles
to stranded bands of mussels
and clearly winter-ringed cockles
tulip shells
and razor clams
ears aching from the bleak wind
eyes half-shut against wind streams of sand
to Swansea Uni College
past the abbey
and today's traffic gauntlet.

A full day looking at yesterday's
storm-drifted algae
from near Mumbles Pier
picking bryozoan colonies from Alcyonidium
and red and brown algae
revelling in this opportunity
to see bladderwrack
and other treasures of the northern hemisphere.

Dyrynda rescues me for lunch
and we speed to the docks
to see the tourist marina
and Impressionist-pastel-hills-blocks-of-flats
and heather
derelict docks
petroleum storage tanks
bulldozed power station
and Lamp Black ruins.

King's Dock
with stationary cranes
and no ship in sight
or even on the horizon
let alone a gang of dockers.

We fish up Bugula Stolonifera
on a rusty cable
from Queen's Dock jetty…
sampling site premiere
for the Uni College mob.

Back to the microscopes for the afternoon
with a minor diversion for coffee
and Gower Peninsula's soil fauna.

Dyrynda again
as I clean up the algal debris.
Into his den
and his seasquirt cultures
biochemistry
film problems
and obsolete freeze-drier:
freeze dry fix your own enzymes.

Off on a wild ride
in the orange Beetle
with unique electrics
through walled and hedgerowed countryside
to see the grounded workboats
at Houghton.

Then further
To Dyrynda's favourite beach
storm waves raging the while:
terrace of old shoreline
rushes up into steep hills and heather;
white farmhouse;
ship ribs on the beach;
blowholes around the headland.

We 'fix' the electrics
and race back to Swansea
for 4X
and Swan
and Toohey's
and a half-pound burger fit for three
accompanied by the latest disco
(including Mitzi nostalgia).

'Home'
to the Times Hotel
past Dylan's Bay View wine and steak bar.
Let in by one who knows I have no key.
Think of writing up Fucus
and Helvetia
and Laminaria saccharina…
but the day was more than all that…
so here it is.

Oxford

Bees and beer at the Head of the River.
Blackwell's world HQ
Ploughman's lunch at a little back street vine-trellised pub.
Illuminated scrolls and poets' manuscripts.
Cook's relics swamping the Pitt-Rivers museum.
Stuffed dodo.
Gardens and Martyrs' Square
crowded out of any historical perspective
    by holiday traffic jams
    and bashers.
Ashmolean's Grecian urns
crying out for a twentieth-century Keats.
Archaeological pillage from the Mediterranean.
Sandstone colleges and academic halls;
worn flags.
Bow-windowed coffee houses;
narrow student accommodation.
Smoke and carbonised grass from summer harrowing.
Literary evening: Ages of Man.
Away to Carterton!
    and a friendly port.

Vienna

it's a great place
all those steeples
icons
friezes
marble statues
with pulsing veins
palaces
earnest intellectuals
psychiatrists
scientists
and boys
not understood
who jump five storeys
on muggy mornings
to say
I
Existed

Paris

Prostitutes
pickpockets
gipsies
beggars
racists.

Notre Dame
Jeu de Paume Impressionists
Montmartre's
Belles Dames Sans Merci.

Polluted Seine
UNESCO
Rodin
history's Guillotines
World War Two bullet holes
Eiffel's garden.

Adieu grey Paree.

Desert Hiroshima

I thought it was France's radioactive iodine
That seared our soursob flowers
And cows
And children's thyroids
But now
I know it's ours.

Maralinga's cloud
Drifts down the years
As Titterton and Baxter
Shift in their seats
But our politicians
Representing the silent majority
Sphinx through their terms of office
Ignoring the bones of the greasy cloud
That rolled across the desert
East of Maralinga.

The Fourth Quarter

The Executioners

The Old Jackals
compound injustice on injustice.
Inevitably
they and their sadistic lackeys
will reap the compound interest
of the wrath of the Chinese people.

Beijing's Martyrs' Square

Who then
speaks for the students and teachers
censored
by bullets in the back
or tank treads as they slept
in Tiananmen Square?

On the spot files of electronic media
shout for the students.
The silent square
shouts for the students.
Martial Law sentries
shout for the students.
The bitter silence of relatives and residents
shouts for the students.
The absence of foreigners
shouts for the students.
Empty bicycles paraded by the Arc de Triomphe
shout for the students.
Obvious lies of 'the official version'
shout for the students.
The Old Jackals' Adelaide doorknockers
shout for the students.

All these silent 'vigils'
shout for the students
of Beijing's Martyrs' Square.

Peace Park, Adelaide, 4 June 1990

Moving tank treads wrote
and having writ
in the blood of the people
in Tiananmen Square
moved on.

No censoring
by the Adelaide City Council
shall erase
the date of it.

Diamonds

Diamonds
of the Torrens Valley's jewel box
seen from Manningham's height
at night.

Diamonds
fairy lighting Geraldton wax
in our Echunga garden
after opening rains.

Diamonds
on dewy grass,
flashing spectral hues
for fledglings
at Mylor campsite.

Diamonds
in your ring
distilling those same pure colours
from a hundred watt bulb,
promising rainbow days
down the years.

Mirror Waters

The second day of spring;
warm and calm
after a week of violent winds and rain.
Warm enough
to burst vine buds
and force me to prune.

Peak-hour traffic
snarled at the dog kennels
and slugged its way
past boiling 'bombs'
to the inevitable semi
bent
on its miscalculated curve.

Home to the view.
Four dams
mirror trees
and apricot sky
down the valley
towards Echunga.
Wakes of ducks
vee dam one
and smudge reflections.

Mirror waters of dam two
silhouette candle pine columns
and grazed cypresses.
Apricot sky
reddens.
Pinatubo's dust
high in the stratosphere
paints a second horizon
highest where the sun set.

Bats ghost past.
A duck
on urgent wings
veers from the house.
An erratic bug
scribbles sky.

God's Necklaces

Hey
God
what's this
necklace
of fisheye lenses
hanging
from my five-strand
clothesline
after
last night's gentle rain?

I see the upside down trees
and sky
of my backyard
and see some fancy stroboscope experiment
as I play
with physics of waves
racing braceleted drops
of fisheye lenses
from my finger
along yellow cords of clothesline
to posts and back.

I shift
to catch a hundred suns
rising
in my fisheye diamonds.

Hey God
I've accepted your gift
and destroyed it
or built on it
with my tampering.

SEG '90 Moves Out, 12 July 1990

Gammons Base Camp
on Doctor Chewing's Creek
east of the gap.
Little corellas flock and fly
low over spiny wattle
thicketing the floodplain.
A later flight
splits and scatters.
Two by two
they settle
in ancient river gums
promising breeding.

Nearer Copley
saltbush greys hills
where miners
long since gone
screed slopes.
Old pine telegraph poles
leaning askew
peg the miles.
Insulators
and relics of soft wire
point and graph sky.

Leigh Creek station.
Chances are
we'll make Copley…
the four-wheel drive
gauging empty
these last twenty miles.

Troubridge Island

strictly for the birds
and wild ocean
moulded in the sand-shadow
of Marion Reef
and the ribs of vessels
foundered there.

Sand cay
stabilised
by boxthorn
and nitre bush
carried in the acid gut
of seabirds
and shat here
to take root
in seaweed banks
and sand
in the lee of the lighthouse.

Hysteresis island
with tails wagging
in life-spanning patterns
of prevailing storms.

Crested terns
colonise and breed
in military squads
of thousands
weathervaning in unison
to the RSM's
bellowing winds.

Cormorants
huddle on spits
hunched
to beat the blizzard
of shifting sand.

Fairy penguins
opportunely nest
beneath the crazily tilting floor
of the slumped powerhouse.

Solar panels
keep the light burning
quietly soaking up energy
like the boxthorns
and nitre bushes
a hundred metres below
more reliably
than bird-mincing props
of wind machines.

Carefully guided groups
edge in,
bare footed
and wet legged
to watch and wonder
then bounce away across the waves
leaving the cormorants
and their boxthorn rookery
to the elements
and ghosts of keepers
and the shipwrecked.

The light flashes white
or red
with its towering partner
on Troubridge Hill
if you are too close
to Marion Reef.

Troubridge Island
settles low on the horizon
and deep in our being
as we plane down
at Edithburgh.

Blue Moon

Roland Robinson's 'gibbous moon'
lit us down the track,
commuting wanderers
from Echunga.

There it was again at night
as we drove the freeway:
low and orange and still gibbous
after Easter's Oakbank fullness
that stirred the jazz bands
and territorial magpies
to blues tunes.

Hack's Valley
draws me out
to moonlit dams
and clearer magpie calls,
the air surprisingly warm
as Roland's moon
rests in a gap in the clouds.

I crunch snails
accidentally
and hear a drumming semi
ply the freeway.
The warning glow of the city
false-dawns the west
silhouetting the supine range
beyond Piccadilly valley.

My old dog
does not even stir
as I perambulate.

Dear Gus

You told me
how you lined up the bottles
on a binge weekend
at Naracoorte
when you used to ride
the big motorbike.

Tonight
I lined up four stubbies
of Cooper's Ale
and thought of you
and your brave mates
lining them up
across the room
and around the corner
and along the next wall.

My cholesterol's a bit high
and I'm told
I drink too much
so I shed a tear
for you
now gone
and me
lining up four stubbies
of Cooper's Ale
and thinking
how naughty
I've been.

Us (To J.B.)

We, together, trust.
You found me foundered.
I found you found me.
We, us, together, trusting.

Autumn Peonies

Cape du Couedic

Morning sun shafts
glare from grey seas.
Waves crash and boil.
Perpetual wind
whines in wires
and bangs the dunny door.
Middens shed six thousand years of sand.

Seals warm rocks
or lie back in the Admiral's pool.
Flowers abound on dunes and cliffs.
Lichens splotch cement water-tanks
and limestone rocks.
The derelict stable
still provides a dry corner for bed and bat.

Silvereyes flit through Leucopogon bushes
and Bradley's nets.
Currawongs move in for a kill
and snare themselves.
Banded, they swear off into the bush
as setting sun yellows waves.

Cape du Couedic Light,
splits and stanchions the night
with black props.
The 1909 doorway
shelters me from the blast.

Cross and Pan
straddle the span of Milky Way.

War Years, Streaky Bay

Blackouts.
Heavy black curtains.
Blacked-out lights on the old Buick;
gas producer to keep the wheels turning.

Recruiting drive gets the boys in.
It looks fun,
with Shirley up in the wings
and collapsing stretchers on stage.
Whole worlds collapse in the next few years.
Some boys come home in their blue or brown.
Others are lost in battles for the Coral Sea
and bloodied jungle.

Coconuts are mailed down from Queensland,
one direct to our pretty schoolteacher.
You don't wrap coconuts.
I'm lucky to be in on the husking,
a big job for Bell Page Primer boys.
The task is done.

The governor comes,
in his whitest of white sandshoes and outfit.
We see war films,
send tins of eggs in dripping to the islands,
get back heavily censored letters
and shop with ration cards.

Hitler crashes.
Pix shows brutal ditches
filled with bodies of the innocent.

We move to Port Wakefield.
The war in the Pacific ends.
VP Day.
The whole school
fifes and drums and flags its way to the baker's shop.
We each get a sticky fist full of boiled sweets
straight from a huge tin.
The Japs got the bomb.

Brother John prangs his Mustang at Labuan
and comes home.
Brother Angus goes on to Japan.
His war goes on for nightmare years.

Marine Archaeology Seminar

Drake comes alive
as I touch his musket balls
flattened against *The Spaniard*
in the heat of battle
and presented here
in the river room
with cheese and wine
and kodachromes
of the *Loch Vennachar* jinx ship
and the raising of the *Lady Kinnaird*'s anchor.

Eight balls from *The Spaniard* too,
and a depression in the plastic foam
where an untreated cannon ball
rusted away
when recovered from the sunken hulk
by this jovial diver
ex RN,
now trapped by archaeological aspects
of Australian wrecks.

I touch your balls again Drake,
and yours Spaniard,
who escaped the Armada battle
only to founder in cold northern waters.

Thanks Scuba Club,
and jovial diver,
for lifting Drake from print
and allowing me
to touch his flattened balls
as I sip wine
and savour Camembert.

Night Dive, Edithburgh

Encumbered divers
lumber down the steps
and plunge into splashing blackness.
Torches shaft the water
and prop snorkellers at the surface.
Nereid segmented worms
snake their way up the beams
to plankton clouds
near the glass.

Greens and browns and reds of marine weeds
surge and sway.
A cuttlefish backs deeper into its algal lair.
Spotted stingray
mimics stone in humped stillness.

Hermit crabs rodent the night,
scurrying around rock faces
where strong currents flow
beneath the jetty.
Sponge crabs
lift their hats
as they promenade the pylons.

Flecked by 'firefly light',
we slowly leave the water.

Peregrine

Neale's 'Golden Eagle'
was greater:
a peregrine falcon
still here
in spite of the DDT
  & Dieldrin
  & E&WS 1080;
soaring
& sitting in a twiggy tree
high above the 'Bidgee
& a million years
  of slowly dissolving caves
  deepening pools
  & solution-pitted rocks.

Neale's peregrine
sits and soars
in its millionth year
despite
thirty years of DDT
  & Dieldrin
  & 1080.
Peregrine falcon
soars
and sits on the 'Bidgee tree
as the USA beef market
commands –

>'Quarantine your DDT
>& Dieldrin
>so we can eat
>DDT-free hamburgers.'

The home market response –
>'We can't afford
>DDT-free
>hamburgers
>or peregrine falcons
>or children.'

Put a sock in it mate.
Pull your bloody DDT out
or feed it to yourself.
I'll settle for organic carrots
or repackaged
DDT-free Oz beef
from the USA.
If it's good enough for the Yanks
it's good enough for the peregrines
>& your children
>& mine.

South Hummocks

Dear Ma,
I saw the old farm
low down across the samphire flats
as I headed the gulf
after savouring Coobowie's marine mysteries.
Swift flow the years,
with so many friends and relatives gone.

My eyes followed the railway line
winding through hills mallee patches
where Soapy trapped rabbits and foxes,
and an old mine shaft
sheltered pigeons,
and a long drop
sweated out of the ground
for some fantasied rainbow.
Less fantastic
the reality of trapping
and sweating of horses and men
at mullock heap erosion level.

Green grew barley
and knee deep clover.
Browned drought.
Swarmed rabbits.
Queued sheep on abbatoir road.

Breathe clean air now
fast
and with love,
enough to last a lifetime,
before smoke palls
from salt brown coal
foul the air
and fly ash floods the saltbush plain
around the proposed power station.

I'm home again, Ma,
but weary,
soul weary.
A midnight hour of gentle rain
heralded by crashing cymbals of thunder
grants me absolution.
I take my sacrament,
a quiet cuppa.

Torrens Bankers

The brown Torrens
swirls its silty way
to the sea…
flushing out water rats
plastics
garden refuse
sticks
and sundry litter.

Waterhens
peck and pry…
tail flicking warning.

Cormorants adjudicate
from a favoured high bough.

I follow crescent tracks
to wet grass.
Mounted police
must have patrolled…
no doubt
searching
for the Brickworks body.

They are a bit early.
It will not rise
until the third day.

Cooper Creek Northwest Branch

I sit on the bank of the Cooper
north-west branch
watching the dawning.
Crows and raptors watch too.

Black cormorants sweep past.
Pelicans Sunderland or galleon by
or pincer their reflected ways.
Yellow-beaked spoonbills
intent on Lake Goyder's greener marshes
fly north in slow hurry.
Corellas leave their crowded bough at crow's insistence
wheel low over the creek with gravelly protest
and return to the same dead branch.
Crow gives up.

Spotted harrier returns to its nest to rest
high in a tall red gum.
Pigeons call persistently
and find each other.
Pelican cruises to Old Coongie landing.
Harrier collects a spray of gum leaves
to line its nest.
Marsh tern passes and repasses,
skimming the water for insects.
Waterhens mind their own business.

Racket of corellas, galahs, and crows,
reminds me of racketty water birds
on croc-etched lagoons in Zambia.

Fish jump in the Cooper.
A yellow rabbit lives the start of another day.
Wagtail hunts mosquitoes.
Thanks mate, after last night's hordes.

Dingoes howled in the night.

Kudriemitchie

Cross sinks low below the coolibahs.
Only one Pointer now,
and the Morning Star.
Magpie and raucous galahs
displace the night owls:
barker, mopoke, and tawny frogmouth.

Water rat prints soft mud
by the dropping Cooper,
north-west branch
here at Kudriemitchie.

Today we plan
to net the Eyrean grasswren
in dune canegrass
near a large lake to the east.
Hence my fire-stirring
star-watching exercise.
Early birdoes join me.
We shift the nets
from coolibah flats to cane-grass dunes.

White-winged fairy wrens
tangled in the nets,
try our patience.
Then the Eyrean bird performs.
We admire
and weigh and measure
and photograph
in my hairy hand.
Eyrean grasswren
with finch beak and wagtail legs
and white and russet flanks.

We release it and furl the nets fast
lest other little wrens
tangle and try us further,
let alone them!

Back to SEG base
with scat in hand.

Smithy's Place

Nine roos
eating grass
at the end of the roo track
I use too,
quietly coming down
through pink gum
and sighing casuarinas
to dwell a day
with your blowflies
visiting swallows
territorial robin
and protesting rosella.

A golden wattle sundew day
as I filter billy tea,
Irish
honey sweet
black.

I mark midday due north
by your shack shadow timepiece.
Sundial rock
tells me now
I've but an hour before I leave,
smelling smoky
from my pink gum fire companion,
the MSc a little further on.

This last hour is for me
and thee and thine
when paddling clay
for building blocks again.

Coongie

Canto I

Early morning crow
scouts the camp from a coolibah.
Six swans trumpet past dawn glow.
Mosquito swarms swap shifts with bush flies.
Dawn orange fades to yellow.
The night's now distant clouds, fire pink.
Corellas squabble raucously.
Magpie-larks beat by as I skirt the dune crest
on sand trilobited by scorpion tracks,
padded and wee'd upon by rabbits,
and graphed by varied wriggly scribble.

A pelican cruises sky.
Crows eat Enchylaena's juicy fruits
and leave me a feather.
Spoonbills sweep paddle bills
through weedy water's edge.
Ducks rearrange their blobby bobbing presence.
Clouds flare red gold near where the sun will rise.

I walk along Mingkulpa Ridge.
Native tobacco,
mingkulpa to the Pitjantjatjara,
left by the Coongie tribe along this ridge,
where they watched thirty-thousand years of suns rise
before their own was set
by white cattle men
near Lake Massacre.
This huge mussel midden
and its *mingkulpa* and flints
say
this was and is and always shall be
Aboriginal land.

Canto II

Cormorants splash down
and expeditioners swim
as the sun rises from Coongie Lake.
I find bone
mixed with mussels and hearth stones.

Red-rumped yellow-bellied parrots
feed amongst *mingkulpa*.

More bone.
Old bullock bones and teeth
mussels and flints
near a major midden.
Iron and stubbies
and a chip of printed porcelain
ominously overlie
the Aboriginal artefacts.

Harlequin mistletoe garlands coolibahs.
Blue Morgania sways near lapping water.

More stubbies
shrimp tails
feathers of water birds
and a Fosters can
are caught amongst the rushes.

I thread through a thicket of moth-wing legume
past harlequined lignum
and dried dung drift algae
to our camp under the coolibahs.

White-plumed honeyeaters
protest from the heart of a cassia
fired for Moses by mistletoe.

Tiananmen Square

The Old Jackals
have run out of Tibets.
Now,
they turn their guns
on their own grandchildren.
The cream of their intellect
flesh of their loins
crushed
in full view of the world's media
in Tiananmen Square.

The Old Jackals have their day.
No official washing will cleanse the facts:
they crushed and ate their pups
in Tiananmen Square.

Tjilbruke Trail

Canto I

Warri Parri
the Emu Dreaming place
where Tjilbruke found the body
of his beloved nephew
Kulultuwi
red ochred
and smoke drying
in his killer's camp
and wrought terrible revenge.

Bullrushes still grow
near gums and weeping willows.
Yabbies, frogs and shrimps survive.
Tjilbruke's fish probably killed
by all these chemicals.
Introduced bees and starlings
compete with native birds and possums
for nesting holes
in dead ghosts of river gums.
Galahs screech and perch.
Kookaburras hunt them away.
Magpies swoop.
Noisy miners investigate.

Emus and his people long since scattered,
Tjilbruke weeps.
Spring tears trickle along the creek
as he bears the body away
for further smoking by the sea.

Canto II: Kingston Park

Tulukudank.
Tjilbruke faces into the wind
as Dowie places him in ancient rock,
weighed down by Kulutuwi's body
and the weight of transgressions
and inevitable retribution
against the laws
that make it possible
for people and land
to live for ever.

Sheoaks sigh
as smoke swirls from the drying fire.
Tjilbruke bears his burden
tears streaming in the wind from the gulf
where salmon have always run
and dolphins hunt.
Tears stream down his cheeks
cold in the wind;
stream down from this dreaming place
amongst the sighing casuarinas
and emu's quandong trees and nitre bush;
weep across the beach into the sea.

Tjilbruke's dreaming place.
The People's dreaming place,
where quandong and casuarinas still grow
and Tjilbruke's tears still flow
as Dowie and legend and law
face him into the wind,
the wind that wipes and hides his tears.
But there they flow across the beach
between the pebbles
of this sacred dreaming place.

Tjilbruke's same wind blows,
blows the nitrous traffic haze
out to the gulf horizon.
Still blows
but cannot hide this city's tears.

Gretchen – RIP, 3 March 1992

Gourmet Gretchen
connoisseur of delicacies
scavenged from compost heap
cow paddock
and old chook house.

Empress Gretchen
reclining in her green beanbag
brown-browed eyes
superiorly surveying
passing cats
and tricycled Trent
who 'tested the water'
once too often.
Ten little pink sausages cycling by
raised Gretch's adrenalin
dangerously high.
Nipped in the bud
Trent learnt the ropes.
You don't take dachshunds
for sentimental dopes.

Devoted Gretchen
on her last day
rose from her beanbag
to see me away.

Down by the chook house
I've laid her to rest
where snuffling and snorting
she razzed many a pest.

Lizean Spitfire

Gawler High's pet steer

Hang in there Lizean,
with your warm breath
flavoured with approved diet
according to Ag course principles.

Hang in close Lizean;
we've fed you and hugged you and loved you.
We loved your big hulk.
We loved your warmth.
We loved your rumbly gut.
We loved your sloppy licks.

Sad day Liz,
in this Agribiz,
you earned a place in the Led Class
in Adelaide's Royal Show '89.

Sad day Liz,
we need your number up
on the hook
in the Dead Class
for the '89 Show.

Fox Glacier, 19 December 1986

Crusty snow breaks
as we crunch away from the ski plane.
Not too far
because of crevasses
but quietly soaking in this top of world
our Antarctic
looking at diamonds
pressing snowballs
and seeing Steve's frost-wedged rocks
dribbling down from black crags.

Feet freeze.
The rest?
Warm enough in 9 a.m. calm.

We loop back to the plane,
our pilot sixth-sensing the weather.
Engines roar as we taxi off.
He jacks up the skis
while circling turquoise pools
of melt water on blue ice,
then slowly spirals down
over arced crevasses
and lateral moraines
to Fox Glacier Strip.

Tenth IBA Conference, Wellington

Weir House
room with a view
looking down onto growing tops of maples
and falling further
to intersections
and city blocks
in pastel buffs, browns, greens and blues.

Harbour waters continue the flatness
of repeating floors of city buildings.
Wellington's hills
leap in wave on wave beyond.

I'm slowly orientating,
but see my south is east
as the sun's glare dissolves the ranges.
At last I find the cable car
but city end
after gravitating past tennis courts
stationers
coffee shops
foreshore limestone sculptures
and seeing porphyra gently surging on breakwater rocks.
Great flat rectangles of reclamation
block in earthquake elevated benches by the harbour.

I return via the gallery
Big Mac's
the shopping quay without water
and cable car
to an early night
after all that perambulating.
The Cross improves my sense of direction.
High on south-east hills
an unseen tower yo-yos a red light.
Sodium lights point and pillar the bay.
Red and white channel markers duet
and slowly miss the beat.
Night traffic and revellers peak and wane.

Wellington waits.

Mismatch

Too many nights
alone
in bed
with you.
Too many nights
alone
in bed
without you.
Too much
aloneness.

Kikuyu

Hey
you kings who build grass castles,
take a closer look at the grass you trample.
See how fine filaments catch the light,
silky white,
each with its little pollen shaker
peppering the breeze with allergies.

Kikuyu lawn,
not all forlorn,
as stalking magpies
probing starlings
grass-pulling galahs
crested pigeons
flitting wagtails
sweeping swallows
occasional philosophers
philanderers
sunsoakers
and tramplers
testify.

Wotzke's Window

Kodak prints
punch leafy patches
through waiting room walls.

Sun streams through the window
shimmers in gum treetops
liquefies North Adelaide's galvo roofs
black shadows St Peter's spires
Impressionist-white-lights Kintore chimneys
shadows the war memorial
sidelights plane tree knobs and twigs
glares me into wall shadows
warms me out of winter layers.

I sit and wait,
relaxing into the watery print
of flooded forest,
almost mangroves.
I'd like to see them Kodachromed.

Lorraine and I

Dear Lorraine,
just when I was thinking of ending
our long-standing relationship
you put on this brave performance:
a hundred buds
and as many full blooms
freshly rained upon;
clinging raindrops
on soft pink petals;
Lorraine Lee pink
because there is none other
quite like it.

Raindrops
magnify waxy leaves
diamond spangled
in the morning sun.

Lorraine,
I've chained my snips and spade.

Signs of Spring

Early almonds
explode in puffs of pastel pink.

Wattlebirds
and a white-plumed honeyeater
quietly sip their dues.

Lorikeets
screech out of red-flowered eucalypts
as I uncoil from weeding beans.

Tongues

Tongues of land
licked into spits
by Gulf currents.

Tongues of dachshunds
soft
warm
clinging.

Tongues of cats
sandpaper rough
licking salt from fingers.

Tongues of cows
rasping unsuspecting torsos.

Tongues of lovers
deep throating desire.

One For Jeff

That lady's tits
are still knocking tops off milk bottles.
Blue tits
on frosty mornings
raising Pasteur's eyes.

Nearly as bad as the president's monkey
putting its finger in it
on the front step
in Zambia.
I blamed the milkman.
Even returned the bottle
and scored a sterile one
from the depot.
Must have been a nut
thinking the milkman's finger
would make such a small hole
in the bottle top.

So if you must have bottled milk,
keep your eyes on blue tits
and finger-licking monkeys
on frosty mornings.

Veale Gardens, 08.50 Hours, 20 May 1991

Time out for twenty minutes.
Homo sapiens stone statues call me over,
but the creek call is stronger.
A pair of Pacific black duck,
supercilious,
flash green wing windows
and paddle in murky water.
Maned duck patrol the bank.

I follow the creek west.
Magpie-lark zaps a giant bug
and belts hell out of it
on the gardener's hose.
I think 'dragonfly',
with that long body;
but then again,
not quite right for dragonfly.
I stalk the bird
and watch it soften up its prey,
stepping on it to hold it down
as it tears off its fill.
I mark the spot
and cross the little creek
to find the dragon's wings.
None to be seen amongst the leaves.
At last:
two dull grey wings of a giant ghost moth
camouflaged in leaves and grass.

On to piping Pan and the Bromeliad House
deliberately missing the sad autumn roses.
One large bromeliad reminds me of Queen's Tears.
Begonias proffer colour
but most is green.

Out to inspect the single sunflower
past the rose garden.
Ginsberg's Sunflower Sutra has to wait
as Lily Marlene entices me along the roses.
Not quite her former glory
but enough to seduce me
despite her lack of scent.
A rose of lighter vein,
satisfies my 'rose nose'.

Ginsberg's sunflower
(or was it Kerouac's?)
takes the stage as I trace its spirals.

Back to business
now that nine has passed.
Red-rumped parrots
continue theirs unconcerned.

Veale Gardens
full of surprises,
doors wide open
when business doors were shut.

Spring Gleanings

Wellington

Baby soap lathers well in Wellington's water
I shut my eyes and feel Mother's hands
massaging my scalp.
My head shrinks to baby size.
I'm one of thousands she washed with baby soap
in her nursing career
securely held as she was taught
and taught in turn.
I blink back to Wellington
and the conference that brings me here.

The Visit

May I, Maya?
May I play your piano?
'Baa Baa Black Sheep'
'Away in a Manger'
'Waltzing Matilda'
'You take the high road
and I'll take the low road'.

May I, Maya?
Waddle your waddly
slap-slap duck
on the wooden kitchen floor?

May I, Maya?
Look at your birthday photos?
Here it comes:
Two burning candles
and rings of kiwi fruit.
Pht!
They're out.
Have a wish.

May I, Maya?
Carry your plastic big-wheeled bike
over your bridge
to the high high lookout
to see the setting sun
follow the moon
into Kingston Park's sea?

May I, Maya?
Look at your toadstools
Quandong trees
pine cones
telephone
and elderly lady with big friendly dog
and positive things to say
about this peaceful end of day?

May I, Maya?
rock your koala rocker
on its enormous spring
and look through your yellow plastic slide
near Kingston House?

May I, Maya?
Lead you home
as first stars twinkle over rooftops
and friendly cat
greets us at the gate?

Thank you, Maya
for sharing with me
this part of your day
now you are two.

Morning Light

Bright morning light
on overhead wires
knifes sky.
Eastward,
dazzling light
skims from car hoods
and tops of wheely bins.
Westward,
blocks of built white
bounce it back.

Swallows,
highwired,
contemplate migration.
Starlings,
fully fledged,
escape their eaves.

I turn the corner
for BP's paper.

Kero Lanterns

computer's still up
despite the power failure
some excuse for 'camping'
got the smell of kero lanterns in my nostrils now
just as well i tried them out for stevie the night before last
we had a real picnic tea out the back
kero lanterns and stars laid on
saw mars and venus and regal and betelgeuse
also the saucepan and the southern cross
don't know what happened to the bats
looked for them over mitsubishi's
but no fluttering sign
can't expect everything
we had ice cream and chicken leg stew
lanterns under the carport
and mum
and the new indian doll
should be more of it
not the power failures
but no doubt we'll get them too

this has been another three mouse day
and there was i
thinking i had got *the* mouse
six mice ago

time to sign off
before we have another power crash
because of all the other buggers
checking out their computers

Scones for Tea

Dear Mum,
got your letter this afternoon.
Recognised the writing when I went to the letter box.
Couldn't recognise the front fence.
It was a dream.
Seemed real,
as I drifted out of sleep.

Looked for a light tea.
Wondered what.
Off sardines
after my suspect damaged tin
and diarrhoea.

Opted for scones.
Looked up the old school cookbook with drifting binding.
Mixed their recipe
with Judy's and yours and mine:
2 cups wholemeal SRF
¼ teaspoon salt
1 tablespoon butter worked in with fingers
2 tablespoons dried sultanas
washed and also worked in
1 cup milk mixed in slowly
dough tipped onto a floured board and kneaded a bit

rolled out with limejuice bottle from fridge
cut into 16 triangles with old kitchen knife
triangles that smile at you as they bake
olive-oiled tray
15 minutes at 220 degrees Celsius.

Numbers are down;
ten left;
the six were spot on for my light tea
chased down with reds
and Tim Fischer's decision.

I'm back on deck.
Can face another night.
Something to be said for scones with sultanas
and a red.

Babysitting Maya at Julie's Place

Outdoors calls us.
Guard dog Peggy follows.
We find pet rocks by the track:
silky black schist
tantalising yellow glints
powdery ochre
no silver or gold.

Chooks forage.
Maya collects the daily egg
pauses for passionfruit behind the shed
explores the tree house and little garden
and throws sticks for Peggy.

We rest on the balcony,
watching.
A big old bushy brown fox
slowly climbs the rocky hill across the creek.
Crouching
with bushy brown tail arched up
it sniffs rabbits down the side of a large rock.
On behind and past the crown of a red gum tree
it pants in late afternoon heat
slows near the crest
stops and scratches fleas
scratches again
then creeps off over the hill
hunting through the night.

'Egg in a hole' for tea.
Then clean teeth, wash feet, into bed and read a story.
We remember the chooks.
I retrieve Chauntecleer from the balcony rail
and reunite him with Lady Pertelote.
Back to your pen Mister Rooster!
None of this bravado!

The big old bushy brown fox
knows too many tricks.
Back to Lady Pertelote,
safely penned.
No night on the tiles
or balcony
rails for you Mister Chauntecleer!

Time for tunes and songs.
Angus comes and goes.
More tunes and songs.
Asleep at last.

The Cross swings up from the dark horizon.
Mum comes home from nightshift.
The big old bushy brown fox
returns to its lair to feed its cubs.

Coming Out

I've come out.
A lot of people have been waiting for it.
I've come out at last.
Must admit it's a great relief.
I've come out
to sit under the carport
and listen to the rain…
long awaited
by garden
and starlings and miners
sitting and shaking wet feathers
in drenched treetops.
I've come out
to enjoy the rain.

Light

scatters from Donna's suncatcher;

diamonds bent tips of seedling grasses
and dewy moss on parapets;

gilds morning's cobwebs and crowns of spinifex;

spectrums walls from bevelled mirrors;

rainbows sky and sprinkler's mist;

scintillates from rippling water;

eddies around aerial roots in mangrove channels;

crescents dappled pavements in sun's eclipse;

dances on doilies through port in crystal glasses;

iridescently colours butterfly wings
mother of pearl
wren
soap bubbles
and oil films on water;

catches russet hair;

paints clouds;

paths lagoon to haloed moon;

lets us wonder.

Adelaide Heatwave Morning

I'm an early bird
directing water where it's needed
to build up reserves
for another forty degrees,
conscious of my drain on city supply
and wondering how long
my little tanks would last
if the system failed.

Time to watch,
remove mosquito habitat
and shift plants in the cool.

Rainbow lorikeets flash past
high and fast
catching morning's orange light.
Pigeon flock twinkles higher.
Starlings,
already bathed in proffered birdbaths,
sit and glisten,
preening on the wires.

I weaken as I water beans
and my list of jobs grows longer.
Playing double rainbows
diverts me
and cools a bit
as heatwave sun
begins to bite my back.

Watering done,
I curtail my ultraviolet exposure
and leave my plants to theirs.

Despite the Rain

Skaife wins the Clipsal 500.
Rain eases
but lights still flicker
as lightning flashes
and thunder crashes and rattles.
I settle for a cuppa in the carport.
Rainbow spans the east.
Starlings shelter in a jacaranda.
A lone male sparrow
opts for complete dry
under a veranda.
Wagtail preens and shakes and dances
showering on an almond bough.
Flying ants rise on tenuous wings
dodging drops bigger than themselves.
Sudden flash and crash
puts wagtail to flight.
Drenched lorikeets wing south.
The 'Five Hundred' stayers are free to party.

Maize Island Revisited

Time warp tunnel:
river gums touch,
arching over the bottom road.
Same causeway,
lignums, spring and bamboo patch.

Speargrass covers the track
Laurie Schneider took
late one night
to rack and back.
We knew he'd do a MacArthur,
it's a one-way track.
He joined us for iced port,
easing us through the irrigation
by his presence.

I walked the seventies' floodbank,
the last hurrah
before the inevitable river takeover.
Brightly fruited
climbing and ruby saltbush
colonise sand
between struggling pear regrowths.
Bees noisily possess flowering river box
bordering block and lagoon.
Burnt out black-gutted red gums
monument the folly of overzealous managers
or careless campers.

Rabbits warren the sandy bank
in currant rack corner.
Trail bikes scar and mar dry lagoon beds.

I head for the rusted-out squatter's tank
on Kokegei's Hill.
Like the old dog,
I rest in the shade of a hop bush.

Rabbits also have rested there.
I find a gin trap
and evening primrose
but no strongly scented purple stocks
without the irrigations.

I walk the weedy mound
marking currant fence boundary
then divert
for cool memories
of pear and apricot trees.
Feet splash down
furrow-irrigated memory lane.
One tall red gum,
from the fifty-six flood crop,
shades me well
where once sultanas grew.

Pink-flowered oleander,
dead native pine,
persistent Geraldton wax,
glaring gyprock fragments,
and concrete floor slabs,
mark the house site.

Up on the sandhill,
sacred site for black and white,
I pass the shady casuarina,
silky oak
and Hofmann's tank stand.
A nineteen-thirty flood box tree
struggles on despite the fires.

Pigsty remnants rust and rot
on heavy soil of the river flat.
Past the killing tree,
mallee ringnecks eat poached egg daisy heads
and fly up to an overhanging box bough
to pick their teeth.

Time runs out.

Wilmington, 19 May 1999

Wilmington pub.
Single globe with shade
suspended from small-corrugation ceiling;
classic;
complete with smoke detector.
Wonder if it's high-pitched
like others above my decibel range.
Ventilator sealed.
Keeps out the cold night air.
Keeps in the CO2
(don't want your CO_2 cosy).

Taffy
broke my Jimmy Woodser solitude.
Did not get to poetry.
Discovered his poem to Mim and Sal
a day later.

Dined with the 'Coolibahs'
flashing poems
and drooling over Pirie gars
flushed by Karinga red.

Late walk
through dark back streets
to see the Milky Way.
You wouldn't believe it.
Scorpion
drowned in the milk.
Couldn't pick Mars
for confusion of stars;
or the Southern Cross.
What is the orientation of the Milky Way
at this midnight hour?

Big rigs
drum north through the night.
Jupiter
seen through street lights
gives me direction.
Map reinforces it.
Odd,
but Scorpio must be sinking *behind* the pub.
I accept the indisputable fact
and enjoy a good Nescafé
made with clear water
read Wang Wei
and count my blessings.
Wilmington's roosters
proclaim their dominion
as big rigs take theirs.

No doubt
fellow guests
hear my kettle's piercing whistle
shrieking mine.
Coffee two
is on the brew.
Jupiter strikes a higher chord.

Dawn.
Orange streaks and scallops
on a green sky
above rippled ranges.
Starlings flock from palms
and forage.
Pedestrian plover
dodges a big rig.
Peewees
break fast on tarmacked insects.
Plover
point-duties the intersection
as sun blazes forth.
Pinhole camera'd clouds
drift *up* the wall…

Supernova 1987A

Full moon.
I'm surprised
but should have known
with Easter here again.

Driving home alone
from G.E. Brown's lecture
on supernovae
and black holes.

Supernova 1987A
seen at Oraparinna
in the Large Magellanic Cloud.

Some prediction G.E.B. made
as he packed up
supernovae study
in late January 1987:
'All we need now
is a supernova.'
Next thing it came…23 February 1987.

Unpack
and hot-wire the world.
Stir up those neutrino detectors
in Japan and Ohio.
Ring the antipodal Ozzies,
Chileans, Kiwis, and Ostrich Eaters.
Scan the plates.
Compare predictions
with rare event facts.
The first supernova seen
for 383 years.
The explosion occurred 170,000 years ago.
Hard work and homework done
pay off.

The witnessing
throws up a black hole puzzle
1.6 x 10 to the twenty-third centimetres away;
2.5 x 10 to the fourteenth grams per cubic centimetre.
Some hard-centred sweet mystery!

Carbon and oxygen and other elemental me
thanks to you
old supernovae.
Who would want more
than to be old cast-off outer matter?
Better that
than black hole core
that can shed no light on the world.

To John Olday

You
are several little pieces
set in the mosaic of my life.
One is conjured now
by the image of Roland's hand
trailing in flowing water
as fig-flower stars
drift by.

Morialta's waters
hurry past
our little casuarina grove
and rush in free fall
down slippery black cliffs
to churn in the shaded pool
far below.
Soft words
trail in languid air.
Drooping casuarinas
melt
in bees' mosaics.

ANZAC Monday, 1999

Dear John,
Been thinkin' of you blokes,
you and Angus and the ol' man,
being ANZAC weekend.

Marched yesterday
for the first time.
Last parade 18 March 1959.
Joined Prospect RSL 8 April 1999,
on the strength of Nasho
first intake 1956.
Could have joined years ago
but didn't know I was allowed.
Joined the Nasho Association too.
All those lone years and complexes
might have been eased a bit.
The price of ignorance.

Too late to march with you lot
but it would have been nice.
Did my first march
with J.L.'s dog-medal
on its sweat-soaked kangaroo-hide string
and his RSL badge
in my pocket
(mine has not come through).
He was not marching
but that's not surprising
since he would have been 104.
He would have liked
the Light Horse Historical Society's horses.
I'm glad I've found the RSL.
Dennis George Brock is Prospect's manager.
He reckons early Brocks lived in peat igloos
long before the name 'Scotland' was invented.

Well, I better go.
Cheers.
Brian.

Peace March 1999

'Lantern Walk!'
I 'stand' corrected by granddaughter Maya,
as I sit on the wall of the fountain.
We are welcomed to 'Kaurna Square'
by the Kaurna 'mayor'.
An odd lot,
as we carry our 'crosses'
and Japanese lanterns
at the 'Kaurna' fountain.
Brolga and ibis look on,
eyes not melted by nuclear fission.
Fifty-four years after that event
we strike our matches.
I wonder how many of the first wave
of occupation forces
are still here,
after striking camp at Nagasaki.
My brother is not.
Thousands of others
saved by the bomb,
still are.

The morrow's paper:
Little Boy and Fat Man earrings
hot stuff at US Atomic National Museum.
Pity about the vaporised Japanese ears.

We Lantern Walk
in fairly silent protest.
Even the loudspeaker
respects the solemnity of the occasion,
losing contact from time to time.

The night turns windy and colder.
Andy, my old biology student,
has a last blast on the microphone.

The stayers process to Elder Park.
More talk.
We break away,
carrying Maya,
and little Peace Cranes,
to the pole in Peace Park
where other cranes wait,
witnessing in the Adelaide dark.

To Shirley Ackehurst

Dear Shirley.
I've been lying in bed
in my mate's shack
overlooking the Murrumbidgee
south of Tharwa,
listening to the rain on the roof
with new intensity
after reading your book last week.

I got my wires crossed
(not unusual).
Went to lipreading class
on the Thursday after the seminar
where I first heard of your book.
No class
but two copies of your book
on the Better Hearing Australia shelves.
I borrowed one
luckily.
Went down with flu
and had three days to read it
before leaving Adelaide.

Today
we've been birdwatching
and listening
across the Murrumbidgee at Angle Crossing
through coffee and waffles at Michelago
and backtracking the hinterland
to Williamsdale and home again.

Some welcome sunshine
so we sat on the sundeck
listening to the birds.
No hope with wrens
but a grey shrike-thrush
was within my range.
I whistled it up a bit
and it came really close
continuing its flutey calling
as I continued mine.

Then the rain on the roof
and cold day's end
with farm dogs barking
homing cars beating the gravel road
currawongs calling
and magpies caroling.

Time for a cuppa.

I can hear my footsteps too…
with my hearing aids.
Discovered that paper *does* rustle
not to mention scudding leaves…
the large ones.
Even heard lorikeets
high in sugar gums.

I'm glad I got my wires crossed
about that lipreading class
and found your book.

Dulcie May Perry

Dear Miss Perry,
Your funereal roses
are slowly unfolding:
deep pink petals
at eye-ball level
near the kitchen sink
where I wash up
and reflect a bit
on the ceremony
and your life.

You obviously enjoyed
Captains Courageous
and *Seven in a Half-Deck*
as you read us chapters
on frosty mornings
at Glossop High School
mid-century.
The mallee fire
beat back the frost,
occasionally exploding out
as limestone nodules
reacted in their inevitable way.
Boys will be boys,
and had to clean up the mess.

'Captains courageous'
sailed their little dories
across the banks again
as I looked for Pacific and Atlantic salmon
in the *National Geographic* fish book.

You requested
we bring one flower
for your coffin.
I selected one
but picked the spray…
intending to snip off the chosen bloom.
Lost the plot
in my 'getting readiness'
and forgot the rose
so used the proffered carnation instead.

Your other request
was also observed
thanks to your further consideration:
> 'Weep not for me
> I see no cause for tears…'

Thanks for this touch too:
> 'Two roads diverge in a yellow wood…'

The Riverland
was ever a yellow wood
when apricot trees and vines
were brushed by autumn.

'Way leads to way' it's true
but even so
our paths touched again
from time to time.
Still I hear your voice
and ever will
sending 'Captains Courageous'
across life's banks.

When I Was Five

Dear Annie,
we had a mission that day
putting flowers on the toddler's grave
the same who followed a while
crying with her cold
as we headed for the jetty.
You sent her back.
Maybe the wind was too keen.
She was buried
just outside the wall
of the hallowed ground
at Streaky Bay cemetery.
We found some flowers:
freesias growing wild,
soursobs and spider orchids.
We knew she went to heaven.

Hunters' Place
Smith's Road, Tharwa

Tinderries

5 September 2000

purple mushrooms
wombat holes
rampant sheep's burnet
giant fallen logs
charred
and crumbling in forty-six-year decay
towering white sally regrowth
saplings block the track

we walk in
past old campsite fire stones
fry pan and toast fork
pellets on the track
sheep or goat?
staring sheep stragglers settle it

we trail down a tussocked swale
beyond a derelict van
to the shed and overgrown sheep yards
a drowned mouse in one of the troughs
and rest in manna's shade

on down the sagging fence line
pig-digs churn forest litter
small blue flowers
challenge our list of names
groundwater seeps through a swamp tea-tree thicket
pig-digs pool clear water
ventriloquist birds
lead us on
the pigs lie in silent ambush
or have gone

lower sun
dictates our slow return
uphill all the long way
we follow the track
past freshly dug wombat holes
scarlet robin and currawongs
and watch sunset across the ranges
blue on misty blue
below the blaze of sun

dusk and darkness press closer
cathartic progress
forest walls echo the lament
moonless blackness of track
and souls misunderstood
cathartic blackness
snail progress
through fog dampness
shearing years

shelling shells
feeling the way
FEELING the way
cathartic FEELING
stumbling in the blackness
but walking out
out of the blackness
out of the misunderstoodness
FEELING the way
FEELING the blackness
FEELING the fog
FEELING the dampness
FEELING the coldness
FEELING the loneness
of catharsis

walking out
out of the darkness
out of the fog
out of the soul lostness
into the rising moon brightness
of summit tundra
walking out
out of the shadows
out of the Tinderries

Murrumbidgee, South of Tharwa

19 May 2001

Hoary frost coats the car
Milky Milky Way;
shooting stars
streak Canberra's false dawn;
young dog barks awareness.
My fingers feel the pinch
so back to bed with my sixty-four-year-old duck;
Joy Toy, made in Australia;
that's a sign of the times;
a bit worn
and with a moth-eaten bill
but far from forlorn.
Roosevelt's Teddy
has nothing on Brocky's duck
floppy headed
stuffed with wood straw
and penguin-winged though it be.

Cootamundra wattle rattles on the roof
as I reflect on a day well spent
counting kangaroos,
fencing,
birdwatching,
and finding Broken Horn and her newborn calf.
We called it Jamie because it was Jamie's birthday.
Broken Horn ate the afterbirth.

No spotted hyenas or dingoes to harass her
but a big old fox
with a white-tipped bushy tail
slunk into a thicket
high above the Murrumbidgee.

Monica's horse
and the one-eyed Hereford bull
enjoyed the luxury of the house paddock.
The horse let us know
it wanted to rejoin the herd.
We opened the gate
and he high-tailed galloped away.
AWOL Herefords
disappeared around the bend
as I beat the rest
and shut the River Gate.

Late in the day
kookaburras called
and cooling shadows
drove me off the heights of the gorge
to the warmth of the hut,
sirloin, wine and talk.

Early Riser

I stir early
and search for the first sliver of new moon.
But this is the wrong end of the night.
Venus blazes forth.
Mars and Scorpio sink.
Magellanic clouds mist the south.
The Cross swings low.
Frost sparkles on the car.
It's too cold for the dog to lift its nose
from its warm coil.
Neale's brave peregrine roosts it out
high above its Murrumbidgee pool.

I've raced the sun.
It's tinted thin streaks of cloud,
distant contrails
and the tip of Mount Tennant.
Venus fades.
Frosty grass crackles underfoot.
A Hereford bellows about separation.
Winging raven, and white cockatoo call.
I climb Raingauge Hill
rub my nose
cover ears
pocket fingers
and feel cold air deep in my lungs.

Contrails resolve into two
as jets west slowly into sound.
Now Mount de Salis's summit's sunlit.

Roos cold-foot it home through frosty grass.
The sun fills a bowl of hills horizon.
Magpies and currawongs glean bogongs.
The dog lifts one eyelid
but stays tightly curled.

I brew a coffee.

Silvery Moon

25 May 2001

I've learnt from Neale:
this sliver of moon in the west is new;
the last sliver in the east was old.

Foxing

30 May 2001

It's a braw morn.
Levitating mist
flows down the valley
and dissipates.
A frozen pipe and plate glass
preclude watering the bull.
The herd is happy enough
grazing frosty grass.
Frost shadows linger in the paddock
as I look for currajongs.
A bird of prey
rests in a yellow-box.
An old fox
ambles up the hill in front of me
stops as I whistle
waits behind a briar bush
wanders on
and noses into a mummified cow carcass.
I skirt him a bit
and flush out another.
Herding roos
I find currajongs
in time for morning tea.

Frank's Place

23 January 2003

Three fire trucks
backburning from Smith's Road.
Frank
worried by 'lights of new suburbs'
flaring over ranges
is genuinely pleased
at D's gift
a cask of white
to help him through the stress.
We broach it
in his barbecue shelter
on the banks of the Murrumbidgee
near the peregrine's big pool,
then back off
past roaring 'Roman candles'
funnelling flame and sparks
into the night sky.

Monday 27 January 2003

Calm
after the night's wild winds
from the cold south.
Hunter cat
drools at rosellas;
waits with the patience of Job
for careless feeders
in the dog roses by Kitty Creek.
I thought he had the eye of a connoisseur:
rosella feathers under the house…
his last kill.

Monday 27 January 2003

A lone wedgie
patrols the unburnt crest of de Salis
looking for refugees.

Wednesday 29 January 2003 (early a.m.)

Tonight's stars
unbelievable
after a smoky day.
Mount Tennant was just visible
three moons of Jupiter
both Magellanic Clouds
a meteor streaks through the Cross
as I turn binoculars on the Jewel Box
fire glow over Kelly's Hill
where brown columns ended the day.

Wednesday 29 January 2003 (continued)

2.50 p.m.

Stinking hot/dusty/smoky.
'Copter at the waterhole.
Fires beyond the immediate ranges.
5.10 p.m.
Thirty-eight Celsius on the veranda.
Strong northerly/dust/smoke.
5.50 p.m.
Fifty-metre fire front on Kelly's Hill.
6.30 p.m.
Cooling down (it's thirty-six degrees).
Monaro Highway's closed.
Fire jumped the river at Cotter's place.
Michelago and Bredbo threatened.
Wutong trees in the house paddock
stark against Canberra's false dawn.
A hand span of fire glow to the south.
Wind change brings six drops of rain.
I'll freeze one
to show the grandchildren what rain looks like.
Tim and Pete bring a tank of water.

Cryptic Rainbows

27 February 2004
Smith's Road, Tharwa

Battered little feather
chewed and rejected
by the killer cat
a gift from the gods
brought on the wind.
I accept it
preen it
and see the spectral lights.

Merino

20 September 2004

The dying wether deserves a eulogy.
It battled on for a week after losing its legs.
Deirdre's proffered bottled water
and niblets of lucerne hay
were gratefully accepted,
attempts to get it on its feet
tolerated
but unsuccessful,
weighed down by long wet wool
and its condition
whatever that was.
It ran with support;
enough to puff me out,
but that does not take much these days.

We saw one crow and two wedgetails
nearby
on our last run to feed and water the patient.
As expected,
the crow had pecked out the live sheep's eyes.
Blood trickled down its wrinkled hairy nose.
Deirdre gave it a farewell rub.
The wedgies had not started their part in Nature's play.

Friends were called upon
to give the *coup de grâce*.
Maybe we ought to have called them a week earlier?

Rhonda's Poem

4 October 2004

roses
raised with love
in Bill's garden
Miffie's retreat
when plotting her next attack
on passing cars

roses
soft petals
cool velvet
on lips and cheeks
carried with love
past the river gate
down the steep gorge
to the water's edge
near the rapids
on the Murrumbidgee

water rushing by
down from the mountains
through three states
and the ACT

roses
love's petals
cast on the water
affirming families
and love
stardust from primordial supernovae
all same stardust we
and rose petals
our children
and the neighbours' children

rose petals
swirling down the rapids
past Angle Crossing
under Tharwa bridge
on through the ACT
slowly disintegrating
into separate molecules
made up from atoms of elements
from primordial supernovae
stardust atoms
flowing on to my taps in Adelaide
where I tend my roses with love
cool velvet petals
soft on lips and cheeks
all same magic stardust we
of Murrumbidgee Gorge and hills.

Neale's Funeral

23 May 2003, 2 August 2003

Dear Neale,
You would have enjoyed your funeral:
honey-coloured solid box –
silver handles
wildflowers and Tim's bronze magpie on it
the elderly priest's regalia
coloured windows
stations of the cross
incense and organ
full house.

Two of your poet mates
read their poems.
Tim read one of yours.
Last supper celebrated.
Your grandchildren carried the sacraments.

No stumbles as we carried you out
to the hearse under the ancient cypress.
The local constable
eased our way
onto the Monaro Highway
for the slow drive past Michelago
to the Pony Club gate
and pioneer cemetery,
last resting place for Garrett Cotter,
first white man west of the Murrumbidgee
teaming up with blacks to survive.
You stole a march on him.

The pick of the views
across the valley to the Tinderries.
Another Cotter dug a true blue hole
in the deep yellow clay.
Your grandchildren played on the pile
and helped fill in the grave
commenting,
'There's room for us too.'

We planted the wooden cross
complete with Christ
salvaged from a demolished church,
and rearranged the flowers.

'Twas Michelago Inn for the wake.
Met your brother briefly,
over from the west.
Also other relatives and friends.
Shared a good red with Old Bill
your nobbleriser mate.
He liked a good yarn.
Then off through the fog
winding up from the Angle Crossing,
still with you, but without you,
to Hunters' Hill.

Hunters' Hill

14 May 2003
12.48 a.m.

It's a warmer night.
I hear a trickle into the new plastic tank.
Not raining now…
so I do a round of the hill.
Drip drip drip at the shed.
I do not investigate.
High-flying planes
hide in the clouds.
Instruments might bring them down safely.
Canberra's glow would help.

Yellow cat and fishy pan
monopolise the doormat.
Drip drip drip on the sun deck.

Slow-combustion stove and Classic FM
warm the living-room.
I read Douay's version
of Saint John on the crucifixion.
It is 'inconvenient'
to be too long dying.
The sabbath
might be violated:
Christ,
Pearl Harbour,
the impatient RN.

It is 'inconvenient'
to be too long dying;
the sabbath might be violated.
I must remember that
when I'm dying.
Perhaps the RN
will remember it
after a lifetime of nursing
if he doesn't have dementia.
Or maybe someone will be kind enough
to put a spear in his side
so the sabbath won't be violated.

Another shower
gently baptises
transplanted cootamundras.

www.ingramcontent.com/pod-product-compliance
Lightning Source LLC
Chambersburg PA
CBHW072151100526
44589CB00015B/2178